Another Day in Paradise

In 1994, children in Sarajevo walk by the broken windows of a building near "Sniper's Alley," a street under frequent sniper fire in the besieged capital city of Bosnia. (UNICEF/94-0864/Roger LeMoyne)

Another Day in Paradise

Front Line Stories From International Aid Workers

Compiled and Edited by
Carol Bergman

Earthscan Publications Ltd, London

First published in the UK in 2003 by
Earthscan Publications Ltd

ISBN: 1-84407-034-4 (hardback)

Printed and bound in the UK by Thanet Press, Margate, Kent
Cover design by Ruth Bateson
Cover photograph copyright © 2002 by James Nachtwey. "Seven-year-old Khairuddin works each day after school collecting chips of wood left over from the fuel for brick kilns. The wood chips are used at home for cooking fires. Location: Kabul, Afghanistan, 2002."

For a full list of publications please contact:
Earthscan Publications Ltd
120 Pentonville Road
London, N1 9JN
Tel: +44 (0)20 7278 0433
Fax: +44 (0)20 7278 1142
Email: earthinfo@earthscan.co.uk
Web: **www.earthscan.co.uk**

A catalogue record for this book is available from the British Library

Earthscan is an editorially independent subsidiary of Kogan Page Ltd and publishes in association with WWF-UK and the International Institute for Environment and Development

This book is printed on elemental chlorine-free paper

for all humanitarian workers,
past, present, and future,
in celebration of their altruism,
and courage

Contents

Foreword

John le Carré

The Rwandan genocide, you will read here, killed seven times more people than the Hiroshima bomb. And the assassins' weapon of choice? Screwdrivers and machetes, of course.

One in five of the world's nations is at war. Two out of five of those wars are being fought in Africa.

Yet the world is governed—if governed at all—by men and women in suits, from air-conditioned offices and limousines, who have never in their lives looked into the eyes of a starving child or walked down a bombed street where the blood is so thick it spoils their nice city shoes.

With every day that passes in our contemporary world, the exercise of great power becomes a game of virtual reality, with terrible and deliberately under-reported consequences for the wretched of the earth. The vast bulk of Western media is so corporatized as to be indistinguishable from the forces it purports to expose. Instead of telling us what they see and hear, journalists in harness to the competing armies of the entertainment industry have become torturers' accomplices, mouthing phrases like "collateral damage" when they mean civilians blown to bits, blotting out the screams and sweeping over the traces in their rush to present their nations' heroes in a pleasing light.

In an era of supposedly unlimited communication, it is the truth-benders and manipulators, not the public, who are the winners. The truth is another country—the one that is inhabited by those brave enough to visit life's hells on foot instead of on the television screen.

The relief workers who in this book bear witness to their experiences aren't saints, but they are members of a rare breed: unedited, unbought eyewitnesses to our collective folly.

Some are what conventional society would call misfits, because the only true kinship they can feel is with the world's victims.

Some, by their own admission, are war junkies who live for the adrenaline rush of the front line.

Others can't rest till they've entered the final heart of darkness without a gun and witnessed the worst of what man can do to man. For them, there is a kind of terrible triumph in witnessing truths that the rest of us hurry to look away from.

Most of the relief workers I have admired in the course of my own wanderings have been by choice nomadic. In contrast to the homeless and afflicted who are their clients, they favor a life of hazard and uncertainty.

But never confuse them, please, with those other so-called relief workers who, thank heaven, aren't represented here at all and shouldn't be: the institutionalized functionaries of global disaster, so integrated with the towering bureaucracy of world aid and so familiar with its weaknesses that they are actually a part of the problem they think they're solving.

What is it that makes this anthology of personal experience in the field so particularly moving? Is it the courage and dedication of the contributors? To a point. Is it their self-humbling in the face of monstrous disaster? That too. But for my money, it's their self-control. It's their suppression of useless pity in favor of doing something practical. It's their determination, in the foulest conditions that man and nature can dream up between them, to make human decency work rather than weep; to do whatever they can, again and again, knowing it can never be enough.

"Did you feed us so we can die with a fat belly?" relief workers in Sarajevo were asked.

What answer could they possibly give? Only, perhaps, that it was better than not feeding them at all.

Preface

This book began over dinner at a small Italian trattoria in Manhattan, far away from the world's continuing conflicts and natural disasters. Sitting opposite me was Iain Levine, a lithe and gentle man, who was Amnesty International's representative to the United Nations. My plan was to interview Iain for a magazine article about humanitarian workers. Several had turned up in my writing workshops over the years, and I had met others socially. I found them compelling, and complicated.

Iain is a nurse whose first job in the field was with Mother Teresa in Calcutta. The son of Orthodox Jews, he grew up in the north of England and speaks with a lilting drawl. Philosophical musings and stories spill out of him rapidly. Then he will fall silent and listen attentively, or ask questions about the New York Yankees, his adopted team.

One of Iain's stories was about Foday Sankoh, the butcher of Sierra Leone. Iain had just returned from that war-torn country, still in the throes of a ten-year tyranny. He had sat with Foday Sankoh in a hut and attempted to negotiate the release of children press-ganged into Sankoh's ragtag guerilla army. Outside the door were scores of machete-hacked victims. "The conversation was deceptively civilized, and the ambience inside the hut was congenial," Iain said. "It was decorated with framed sentimental aphorisms copied by hand from Hallmark greeting cards."

This was one of many telling details Iain recorded in his journal and repeated to friends and colleagues during countless debriefings and e-mails. Transforming execrable lived experience into a narrative is one of Iain's tools for staying sane, a device that enables him to keep working, to feel that his efforts have meaning and results. It is also a témoignage, a witnessing, for the historical record.

For months before we met, Iain was taking his writing a step further. He had enrolled in a one-day writing workshop and was inspired to begin a book about his twenty years in the field. An avid reader, he admires the Polish journalist Ryszard Kapuściński and wanted to use his personal kind of storytelling as a paradigm. Did I think this was a good idea? I did, and I wanted to see what he had already written. He pulled "Another Day in Paradise" out of his briefcase. My own intention—journalist writing about humanitarian workers—felt like an appropriation and evaporated. Iain's manuscript was a gift; I would compile and edit an anthology of stories by the workers themselves.

This has never been done before, and the reasons are self-evident; the logistics alone are daunting. Humanitarian workers are scattered all over the world, often in remote and catastrophic landscapes. Satellite phones and e-mail connections are possible but not always secure. A story from the Sudan had to be abandoned for fear of endangering a clinic; the only available e-mail service was via a radio link, easily accessed by the Khartoum government. Whether the workers are in the midst of emergency rescue/relief operations or in quieter development-oriented postings, they are hard to reach, and they are very busy.

There were also other problems: Some aid agencies were reluctant to cooperate. Others understood that to allow their humanitarian workers a voice was an opportunity to reach potential donors who are weary of mail solicitations and soft focus photographs of starving children. But, in return, they wanted to maintain control of the text. My powers of persuasion were severely tested.

Oxfam (US) was the first NGO (nongovernmental organization) to compile a list of workers to contact who might be

Unregistered Afghani refugees line up for aid at the Peshawar offices of the United Nations High Commissioner for Refugees. (UNHCR/31075/11.2001/A. Banta)

willing to write stories, no strings attached. Others followed. Others continued to have doubts about security issues or public image. The International Committee of the Red Cross (ICRC), headquartered in Geneva, was unusually coopera- tive. I caught them at the right moment, just as they were rethinking their relationship with the media. They invited me to attend four days of a training sequence for new recruits and those already in the field.

The book was nearly complete by the time I arrived at the ICRC conference center in the summer of 2002. All the controversial issues I had been grappling with as I mentored the stories in this collection surfaced during those few days and were reframed. Though I was not allowed to interrupt the sessions with questions or take photographs, I lived communally with the workers, many of whom had worked in the international disaster relief system for other agencies in the past. Chatting informally over drinks and meals, I learned more from them than all the books I had read and conferences I had attended for two years. My enthusiasm for the project deepened; so, too, my respect for the humanitarian workers. These are the people, many so very young, risking their lives on the ground while politicians and diplomats negotiate in velvet-curtained rooms.

Most humanitarian workers begin their careers in their twenties, oblivious, at first, to the controversies about humanitarian intervention in the UN Security Council or the corridors of foreign-policy institutes. Raw and energetic, they turn up in the world's trouble spots as paid or unpaid volunteers for an NGO or a UN agency. These newcomers are given a lot of responsibility: they drive and maintain land cruisers, negotiate with soldiers at roadblocks, distribute money to local employees, order and distribute supplies, report landmines and organize their defusing and disposal, set up field hospitals and schools, tend the wounded. Before long, humanitarian work has become their passion.

Asked about their courage and motivation, most deny they are courageous or altruistic and reject an outsider's romantic notions of their work. They are in it for themselves, for their own gratification, most say. Or because they cannot stand by and watch people suffer. They assume this is a normal response. Doesn't everyone feel this way? Shouldn't everyone feel this way? It is hard for humanitarian workers to understand that their lives are dangerous and devoted in ways most of us cannot imagine.

At any one time, depending on the upheavals in the world, there are several thousand humanitarian workers in the field. They come from many countries, though Europeans and North Americans are over-represented. Known as expatriates, or expats, in the countries to which they are sent—as opposed to locals that are hired on the spot—nationality is almost irrelevant to them. Indeed, it is a great irony that expatriate humanitarian workers are transient and international by choice, whereas their clients—refugees and internally displaced people (IDPs)—want nothing more than to go back home or be settled in one secure place. Humanitarian workers, in general, have a different notion of home and security. They often complain, jokingly, of the pressures of a "normal" life and admit to enjoying, or needing, the adrenaline rush of the front lines. They come in from the field to rest and refresh themselves or to take a job in the back offices of the organizations they work for, if they can get one. In time, they become restless and take another field assignment, and then another, and another. They seem to retain their vigor for about two decades, until they collapse from burn-out or decide to return to their country of origin and begin a family. Like soldiers, they have witnessed brutality and devastation, the worst of humanity, the worst of what we have done to ourselves. Some cannot erase these images from memory, or dreams, and suffer from post-traumatic stress disorder in varying degrees. This agony is real, and common; you will find it here in this book alongside the joys and gratifications of humanitarian work. Most impressive is that even those who have been traumatized transcend their fears while still in the field, seek counseling when they return home—offered by most of the agencies these days—and continue to work. It is only a few who cannot go on or regret their choice of profession.

In many ways, an anthology is not representative; nor can it be completely balanced or inclusive. Solicitations for stories went out in many forms and through many channels: e-mail broadcasts, word of mouth, flyers at conferences. As editor, I could only work with what was offered; not everyone was willing or able to interrupt his or her work to reflect and write. A few stories were abandoned half-finished, or were simply not workable, or came in past deadline. For the most part, however, once a worker committed to writing a story, he or she stuck with it to the very end, even if this meant weeks of revision via e-mail or over coffee in London or New York. The result is an anthology that is gripping to read and startling in its contribution to the discourse about humanitarian work.

Carol Bergman
New York City

Part One

Natural Disasters

Evidence of drought, a dead cow by a roadside in Chad. (UN Photo 164693/John Isaac)

We begin with four stories about humanitarian response to natural disasters: famines in Sudan and Chad, a flood in Vietnam, and a volcanic eruption in Ecuador. This is but a small sampling of natural disasters, or natural hazards, as they are called in the aid business. Others are hurricanes, typhoons, cyclones, wind storms, earthquakes, insect infestations, extreme temperatures, droughts, landslides, epidemics. The entries on this list, culled from a UN report generated by the ISDR (International Strategy for Disaster Reduction), sounds like a litany of biblical plagues.

That said, one wonders whether the word natural is always accurate. Sixty-one percent of all "natural" disasters from 1980 to 2001 were linked to global warming, mostly a human-made disaster. What we have not made, we exacerbate. In 1998, the Limpopo river flooded in Mozambique, a country already crippled by years of civil war. In 2002, a volcano erupted in Goma, still in the midst of war. Emergency preparedness, in the conventional sense, is not possible in a country at war or in a countryside so poor, vulnerable, and underdeveloped—once again in the aid agency jargon—that it has no work or schools, much less an emergency-preparedness infrastructure.

Enter humanitarian workers, sent to assuage the suffering. They are in the field to distribute rations, build shelters and latrines, tend to the wounded, facilitate the delivery of clean water, repair roads, establish temporary schools, enlist victims to participate in their own recovery and future. They do this with gusto, grace, and commitment. The family swept away by the flood might be their own.

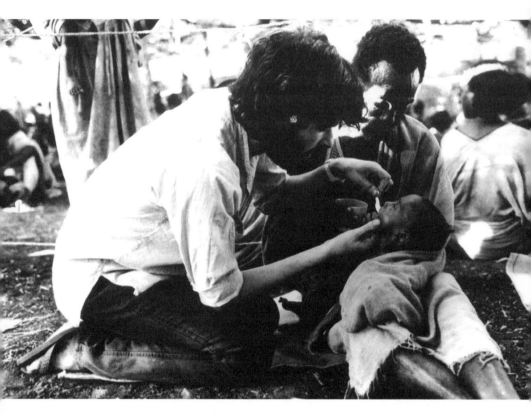

Iain Levine working in the feeding station at Wad Kawli, Sudan, 1985. (Courtesy Mike Wells, for Save the Children, UK)

1 *Another Day in Paradise*
Sudan

Iain Levine

"I sat with him trying to encourage him to feed his child, spoon by spoon, hoping to show by gesture and smiles that this was good for his baby, that it was the only chance the baby had to survive."

Prologue

My parents have a picture of me taken in Wad Kawli, Sudan, in 1985. It contrasts strangely with the domestic coziness of their living room, where it sits. In it, I am kneeling down, holding up a spoon to the mouth of a tiny baby lying in its father's arms. I remember nothing of the baby, not even whether it lived or died, though when I examine the picture closely, it's hard to imagine how it could have lived in such a harsh climate and with such rudimentary facilities.

While the baby's face has disappeared from my mind's eye–swallowed up by hundreds of other pinched baby faces that I saw at that time and over many years–I still recall the father vividly. His wife had died on the long, dangerous journey on foot from Ethiopia, and he was left with his baby and a handful–three? four?–of other children. They would hover at his shoulder, silent and unsmiling, as he sat, cross-legged and calm, with the baby in his arms. I sat with him trying to encourage him to feed his child, spoon by spoon, hoping to show by gesture and smiles that this was good for his baby, that it was the only chance the baby had to survive. He smiled back and mimed his thanks and appreciation at all that we were doing, and I smiled back again and handed him the spoon and said, "Now you do it."

Ten minutes later I looked back and, once again, he was sitting there, impassive, staring ahead, with the baby in his arms and his other children standing over him, the cup of milk and spoon forgotten. I wondered what he was thinking about—his dead wife? His village and farm left behind? Or, perhaps, he was just waiting for his baby to die. The sanctity of life is one thing, but in the harsh and unforgiving world of an Ethiopian peasant farmer, caught up by war and drought, there is only so much energy, so much food to go around. In his mind, I am convinced now, he already had let the child go. And despite my tireless efforts, he was just waiting for it to die.

Morning

I wake at 5 a.m. with the sun streaming onto my face. I'm lying under a mosquito net in my tukel, the roughly built, wattle-and-daub circular hut that is my home. Instinctively, I reach my hand out from the net to turn on my shortwave radio for the BBC news. The familiar strains of the signature tune—dadu da da da da dadu—remind me of a far-off world. "Our" disaster—aid workers soon become very possessive about what they do and where they work—is featured on the news, third item. The report describes aid workers as "tireless," and, as always, I groan and wish that they would leave out the heroic descriptions and just call us exhausted. Sleepily, I stumble out into the sunlight and toward the shower—a barrel of water with a spray tap punched into it—and hope that our cook will have the tea ready.

Forty-five minutes later, we're heading along a dusty road toward the refugee camp. Camp is such an inappropriate word, bringing to mind a group of Boy Scouts and half a dozen tents in a bucolic English field. With a population of seventy-five thousand people, it's the size of a small town. We're a hundred and fifty miles from the nearest paved road, electricity, running water, or phone. The air shimmers in the

Workers pick up food supplies air-dropped by the World Food Program, Thiekthou, Sudan, 1998.
(UN/DPI Photo by Eskinder Debebe)

heat, even this early in the day, giving the camp a misty appearance and making it seem unreal. From a distance it seems quiet. Except, of course, for the droning of the flies.

My feeding center is built from poles and straw mats that keep the harsh sun off the kids but not the dust that blows in on the hot breeze. It's already almost full with nearly five thousand children, sitting patiently, too patiently, with their mothers or fathers or older siblings waiting for the first meal of the day: an orange plastic cup of hot, sweet milk. As I get closer, I see some of the refugee women, sweat pouring down their faces, mixing huge quantities of oil, sugar, and milk powder in huge vats over wood fires. Two donkeys trot up and start to chew on the straw mats that make up the wall of the feeding center. The guards dispatch them harshly with some well-aimed blows to their bony flanks. Disconsolately, they trot off in search of greener pastures. However, it hasn't rained in months, so there is hardly a green leaf to be seen, just miles and miles of flat, barren land.

Huge, succulent, and dark blue, the flies are everywhere: on the faces of children, in their cuts and wounds, in the spilt milk, shit, vomit, and blood. In the harsh and intense sunlight they reflect the colors of the rainbow on their obscenely huge bodies. Worse is the noise they make, an incessant buzzing, around the face and eyes. And the more I sweat, the more they seem to like me. The people are dying like flies here as the flies breed and proliferate.

We have arranged the children in long rows facing the entrance to the feeding center, the sickest and most malnourished near the front where, as the nurse in charge, I can keep an eye on them. The healthier, mostly older children sit at the back. The smell is overwhelming, a mixture of sweet milk and unwashed clothes and bodies.

I had first seen this scene I was now living, or something vaguely like it, some months previously on BBC TV. I was working at a children's hospital in London. I loved the work, but having just returned from a year in India, I was restless and dissatisfied. I was seeking something more challenging and more intense. Then the 6 p.m. news came on the TV on the ward. I was transfixed by the images of the malnourished children in a feeding center in Korem, Ethiopia, their intense gazes out of old men's faces, the almost complete absence of tears. I was intensely jealous of the relief workers who were shown on the film. Not that they were being featured on TV, but because they were there, where I wanted to be. Suddenly, the sweet little three-year-old in my arms–blonde, middle class, pudgy, and with a slight asthma attack–seemed gross and overweight. I turned away from the screen. And, feeling more than a little guilty, put the little boy back into his cot.

Of course, what was missing from the TV images was the hideous sound of the flies.

Now I am here, and my first task of the day is to see how many of the children who came yesterday have returned. I check out the front row and notice immediately that Gebraselasse, who was just hanging on yesterday, is absent. I spent a lot of time with him and his mother and had thought that he might make it. I immediately call over one of our home visitors and tell her to go to his tent to see if he is still alive. She returns a few minutes later with the news that I was expecting: He died in the night. She arrived at his house just as the family was leaving to bury him.

Afternoon

This afternoon, within the space of fifteen minutes, two children died in my arms.

On each occasion, I am called over by their mothers. Though I understand hardly a word of Tigrina, it is clear what they are saying.

The children lie strangely still. I can see the skin between their ribs move in and out as they struggle for breath. Their eyes are dry and unseeing, their hands and feet feel cold to the touch despite the heat. I hardly have time to do anything, though, in truth, there is nothing that can be done before there is a sigh and it is all over.

I am glad that I don't speak a word of their language and that they don't understand mine. What can I say to the mothers? I hand each of them a scrap of white cloth for a shroud and point to where to bury the body. Then on to the next child.

In fact, the death rate of the camp is well down from the early days. When I first arrived, a measles epidemic had just broken out. With a desperately malnourished population and terrible overcrowding, it was inevitable that the disease would spread unchecked. At its worst, we had a hundred deaths a day. We hired one of the refugees to count the funerals. From sunrise to sunset he sat on the hill overlooking the makeshift cemetery using a cheap notebook with two columns drawn in it. In one column he made a cross for every child death and in the other for every adult death. For weeks he was the busiest man in the camp.

Midway through the afternoon a journalist comes by the feeding center. She's wearing one of those quasi-military khaki waistcoats with dozens of pockets, and you can tell that it's all one big adventure for her. I suppress a smile and resist the temptation to ask what she actually puts into the pockets. Her questions are predictable and unimaginative. For what seems to be the hundredth time, I try to explain how it feels to watch a child die. Then, tiring of my own formulaic response, I lead her to a small child who has little time to live. Pointing to him, I ask her what she feels. She stares at the child for a long time but says nothing. I notice that there are tears in her eyes. Feeling ashamed of my cheap gesture, I start to speak more gently and try to explain that we don't think of those who die but those who live. I show her a child—bright, alert, smiling on his mother's lap—and explain that six days ago, he had come in sick, dehydrated, and malnourished. Now, he's well on the way to recovery and, every time I look at him, I feel a surge of excitement and satisfaction because I made that happen. I tell her that aid workers, like children, drunks, and gamblers, still believe in the possibility of a perfect world, though, even as I say the words, I don't know if I really believe them or if I'm just saying them because they sound cute. However, I can see that I'm not really making much sense to her, so I excuse myself to attend to one of the children.

As night falls I watch the children and their families go home, carrying their blankets and a cup of milk or porridge for the night. The women are extraordinarily beautiful in their embroidered dresses and elaborate hairstyles, and I

In a dispensary run by Save the Children Fund in Sudan, supplementary feeding is administered in a settlement for Ethiopian refugees. (UNCHR Photo 14089/C. Penn)

marvel at their quiet dignity and proud bearing in the midst of so much enormous deprivation. The procession gradually disappears into the horizon as I wonder which ones will not come back tomorrow.

Evening

Back at our compound, after dark, we calculate the impact of hot, sweaty days in the feeding center as height and weight percentages are measured and changes noted. When a child arrives at the feeding center, he or she is measured and weighed and, on the basis of these figures, the weight for height percentage is calculated. One hundred percent means a normally nourished child. In these circumstances, 100 percent is so rare as to be abnormal. Under 80 percent is usual, under 70 percent, unremarkable. I once saw a child that was 55 percent weight for height, so fragile and slight it took my breath away.

Any child under 80 percent is admitted to the feeding center. Children under 70 percent are admitted to what we grandiosely call the therapeutic feeding program; this means two extra cups of milk a day and a seat nearer the front so we can watch more closely. Today we weighed every child, most of them screaming, on the hanging scale and then, like Dickensian clerks, noted down each calculation in our huge ledgers, working out which children can be discharged and who will require more attention.

To the sound of Sade's "Diamond Life" conversation meanders over the meaning of life. What makes a just political system? Then some gossip about the day—the cook fired for stealing milk, the new love affair between our logistician and one of the nurses from another organization working in the camp. More discussions about love and life and sport and letters from home. Robin complains that she hates "fucking camping," but nobody takes her seriously. Tonight there's a bottle of arachis—distilled date liqueur—which is both illegal and practically undrinkable; its fiery taste eases the pain of the day, and I soon forget about the two children who died in my arms. Instead, I gaze admiringly at our new midwife, dark-haired and pretty, and wonder if an occasional smile in my direction is really meant for me.

And, joy of joys, no flies to disturb the calm.

Night

It's cool now—or as cool as it's going to get—and time for sleep. Too lazy and tired to look for the boiled and filtered water, I take a cup from the barrel and brush my teeth. I'm risking giardia or hepatitis or any one of a million dangerous tropical diseases, but I'll take my chances. With a flashlight I carry out my regular nighttime search for wild life. Though it's dry season now, these flashlight inspections of the hut, my bed, and my shoes have become a nightly routine. At the start of the monsoon season the rains flooded my tukel, turning the dirt floor into a sea of mud and attracting a menagerie of poisonous wild life; snakes, scorpions, and camel spiders became my reluctant companions, though the reluctance was more mine than theirs.

Now I lie naked under my mosquito net, sweating in the still, humid air, listening to Van Morrison's "Tupelo Honey." "She's as sweet as tupelo honey, she's an angel of the first degree," he sings, in his gravelly voice. No honey for me tonight, though I'm too tired to care. I try to read my *New York Review of Books*. It arrives regularly, though usually six weeks out of date. The contrast between its exquisitely honed intellectual, New York sensibility and the realities of my daily life is a source of fascination and frustration. Its esoteric obscurity often infuriates me: Are these issues that intelligent people should be worrying about? I am strangely drawn to the idea of a space where ideas matter and where writers and readers engage fiercely and passionately. I turn first, as always, to the personal ads, which are full of tall, beautiful, smart, witty, elegant, successful, intelligent women whom I shall never meet. I wonder whether I should bother replying to any of them, but I'm too young, too poor, and too far away. Sighing just a little, I drift off to sleep and dream of sophisticated New York City women, a time and place where electricity and healthy babies are the norm, and where insects and humans all know their place.

2 *Awakening*
Ecuador

Henry Gaudru

"I use my scientific knowledge to protect people who live in the shadow of volcanoes and to help them plan for the future, given what we know about the volcano's activity."

On the night of November 13, 1985, about twenty-six thousand people were killed by the eruption of the Ruiz volcano in Colombia. These people would not have perished if they had walked a short distance from their homes to higher ground. Why didn't they do this? Why didn't they know they could do this? The answer to these questions is complicated. An international team of well-qualified volcanologists had, in fact, studied the coming eruption of Ruiz for over a year before the disaster and had prepared accurate maps showing threatened areas. Their survey was presented to the local government, but nothing was done. Personally, I was very frustrated when I studied this historic tragedy, and also sad. Good science is not enough, I thought to myself.

I fell in love with volcanoes when I was a teenager on a trip to Italy. Mt. Etna erupted while I was there, and I was intoxicated. When I returned home, I read books about volcanoes, watched films about them, and later studied geology and volcanology. Volcanoes are a window into the earth's interior, and this fascinates me. For centuries, millions of people have been terrified and attracted by their power, and I am no exception. In ancient myths volcanoes are gods or inhabited by gods, revered, worshiped, and feared as gateways to

Henry Gaudru before a live volcano in Cape Verde in 1995. (Courtesy Henry Gaudru)

hell, invoked by poets and storytellers. People continue to live close to volcanoes; the soil is fertile, the landscape breathtaking, and the mysterious and ferocious power of the mountains remains elusive and enthralling.

Today, I am a volcanologist, but I am also a humanitarian worker; I use my scientific knowledge to protect people who live in the shadow of volcanoes and to help them plan for the future, given what we know about the volcano's activity.

Most eruptions are preceded by premonitory signs, which, if recognized and heeded, can give timely warning of impending events. These signs may be subtle or complex; detailed study is necessary to interpret them accurately. Some of history's greatest catastrophes have been caused by eruptions whose early signs were unrecognized, misunderstood, or ignored.

I AM BASED in Geneva, thousands of miles away from most volcanoes. From the safety of this vantage point, we monitor volcanic activity all over the world. We remain alert and are poised to leave quickly as news arrives about an awakening of long dormant volcanoes or an increase in eruption of an active volcano. In October 1999, after about eighty years in repose, the Tungurahua volcano in Ecuador, a land of volcanoes, was on orange alert, one notch down from the most dangerous–red alert–threatening a major eruption. More than thirty thousand people live in the area at the foot of the volcano.

I called the IDNDR (International Decade for Natural Disasters Reduction), a UN agency, also based in Geneva, to tell them about this eruption and to suggest that I travel to Ecuador to consult with the local scientists. I contacted my Ecuadorian and French colleagues to obtain further details about the activity, and I read up on the volcano's prehistoric and current history, including the intervals between active and dormant periods. One week later I received a UN contract for a mission to Ecuador.

BEFORE LEAVING for a new mission, I don't know whether to feel worried or happy. My wife urges prudence, because she knows that, if it is possible, I will probably get very close to the vent of the volcano, and that this is dangerous. In 1991, two of my friends, Maurice and Katia Krafft, and their American colleague, Harry Glicken, were killed by a particularly large pyroclastic flow during the eruption of Mt. Unzen in Japan. In January 1993, during an international scientific field trip within the active crater of the Galeras volcano in Colombia, a sudden and violent explosion occurred. Six volcanologists were killed, and there were several other injuries. Following these tragic events, new recommendations were compiled by experienced volcanologists to mitigate risks, but this does not mean that we are not at risk. We are at risk, we know this, but we continue working nonetheless; the scientific data we gather can save thousands of lives.

I take personal clothing, a video camera, as well as special equipment–a helmet, a gas mask, heat insulation gloves, and mountain glasses to protect my eyes from volcanic dusts. Scientific equipment varies with each mission and the type of eruption, the elevation of the volcano, and where it is located. Once in the presence of the volcano, I need my eyes, ears, nose, and brain; intuition and knowledge are as important as any scientific equipment. I can note changes in de-gassing and steaming, the color of the plume indicating variations in the composition of the gas, the emergence of new steaming areas, the development of new ground cracks or widening of old ones, and changes in the color of mineral deposits on the face of the volcano. A wide variety of sophisticated instruments will allow necessary additional data to confirm visual observations from a distance if the eruptive activity is too severe.

APPROACHING ECUADOR, we cross the Andes in a cloud. But as we drop over Quito, we are above a sunny city, a long narrow shelf that expands north and south. The flank of Pichincha, another active volcano, looms to the west. Low hills fall away sharply to a valley bottom with the eastern arm of the Andean cordillera in the far haze. This is an impressive landscape, and it stirs me; I feel as though I am peering into the past. As with most of the earth's mountains, valleys, and plains, the Andes have been slowly sculptured by uplifts and erosion over millennia. Often, while gazing upon these natural wonders, I remember that nothing is permanent on the earth, all is change, all in balance. Volcanic eruptions, despite their dangers, are essential to the evolution of life.

THE FIRST MORNING in Ecuador we head for Pelileo, a small town located about fifteen kilometers north of Tungurahua. Near Latacunga, the perfect cone of Cotopaxi is illuminated by the sun's first rays. This giant (5,897 meters) volcano, believed for a time to be the second highest mountain in the

Ecuadorian women, one with a baby strapped on her back, cultivate a field on a mountainside.
(UNICEF/HQ91-0027/Maines)

world, was climbed by both Alexander Humbolt and Edward Whymper. In a land of volcanoes, Cotopaxi still stands out as a monument to humankind's attempt to conquer nature.

Ecuadorian and French colleagues are already working in Pelileo as we arrive. Together, we examine the latest seismic parameters and share our opinions. Darkness falls in the quiet night. Like a cannon shot, the volcano rumbles and then explodes. A few seconds later we feel the shock waves. Incandescent light rises above the crater and lights up the sky. Though I have seen such eruptions many times, I am awed and frightened. Throughout the night, from the terrace of our hotel five kilometers away, I watch the volcano and hear its roar. Throughout the night it does not rest.

The next morning, after a brief sleep, we are up early to drive to a small mountain facing the volcano. Our task today is to measure the gas. We can do this at a distance with special electronic equipment. A large plume rises above us as volcanic ash carried by the wind falls into the valley and onto the flanks of the mountain. One hour later our measurements are finished, and we inch closer, entering the restricted zone two kilometers from the summit. It is guarded by two Ecuadorian soldiers. A few hundred meters further and we are faced with a wooden marker, a skull and crossbones etched into its rough surface.

What had once been a fertile area is now gray desert, covered with ash as fine as talcum powder. The air is hazy and still–the villages emptied in an evacuation–and eerily quiet. The mountain road between Riobamba and Banos at the foot of the volcano has been closed for several weeks, and ours is the only vehicle in sight. We continue slowly, crawling through the dust.

We present our permit to the guards at the military road-block near Banos, a ghost town with its shuttered stores and abandoned houses. We examine the thickness of the ashfalls on the roofs, in the streets, and in the air. When the ash particle level is in excess of the ambient air quality standard, there is a health risk to asthma sufferers and patients with severe cardio-respiratory disorders. The gas emissions are also dangerous: Sulphur dioxide is an irritant, and hydrogen sulphide is highly toxic. We conclude that Tungurahua is a high-risk volcano and, if it erupts fully, it will threaten many people.

Overhanging the abandoned city, the crater is still smoking. We stay for about an hour, alone in this primeval world. Every house still standing is cloaked in a thin layer of volcanic cinders.

Finally, our measurements and observations complete, it is time to leave. Past the city limits, past the roadblocks, a crowd is gathered, and the people are angry, desperate. They don't understand why they cannot return to their homes immediately, why this is forbidden to them. Or why we have been permitted into the village. It is a difficult and scary moment. The villagers are very upset, and they blame us, shaking the car, shouting, banging on the hood. They cannot perceive the danger or accept it. Many are poor people with a parcel of land and a modest home. The volcano is spitting ash. This is nothing, they say. Where is there evidence of a major eruption? Why has the evacuation been ordered so precipitously? We try to explain, but our scientific explanations are inadequate. The results of our data collection do not assuage the fears of the villagers or the reality that they might lose their homes. Though my Ecuadorian colleagues speak to them in Spanish, and I speak a little Spanish, we do not know if they have understood us: There may be a major eruption, it is not certain, we agree that evacuation is necessary. Until the volcano calms down, they cannot return home.

Both the people and the volcano are now restive and demand our attention.

I REMEMBER when Mt. Cameroon in Africa erupted in March 1999. One thousand villagers were evacuated as walls collapsed and lava flowed. When my team arrived, it was necessary to ask the local sorcerer's and medicine man's permission before climbing the volcano for our scientific investigations. Moreover, we had to dance and offer gifts of coins to the angry gods. Although the people did not understand our task very well, they accepted what we were trying to accomplish in aid of their safety and survival. Perhaps it was our collaboration with the sorcerer and medicine man that helped us there. In Ecuador we did not have this option. Three months

Tungurahua volcano, seen from the town of Pelileo, Ecuador. (Henry Gaudru)

after the evacuation several Banos residents bypassed the military checkpoint and returned to their homes to plant crops and tend their farms. There were some violent skirmishes, followed by a decision by the Ecuadorian government to institute an early warning system instead of a full evacuation. I hope that the permanent monitoring already running and the additional equipment installed following our mission will be efficient enough to alert and evacuate the population before a terrible event.

In truth, one cannot abandon or prevent settlement of the areas where volcanic hazards exist; what is important is to learn to live with them as safely as possible. We try to be accurate and to predict the future of the volcano, if possible. We urge the local government to read our reports carefully and heed our warnings. We hope it will make sound decisions on land-use planning and public safety.

3 *Grandmother*
Vietnam

Ngan Thuy Nguyen

"The stream of news flashes about flood refugees triggered unparalleled anxiety in me; these refugees could very well be my family in Vietnam. Images of Grandmother scooping floodwater from her house tormented me."

Just as I'd imagined, Grandmother is lying on her army-green hammock perched between the two poles guarding her front porch. Like a small child, I run toward her with my backpack sloppily rolling off my shoulder, screaming, "I'm home! I'm home!"

"Holy God and Buddha! Is that you, Ngan?" she gleefully cries, as she disentangles herself from the hammock and stumbles toward me. I smell her familiar betel-nut breath and the eucalyptus oil on her sore muscles. We embrace tightly, our round cheeks wet with tears. The pangs in my stomach return as I feel the longing sensation of home. Grandmother's right eyebrow lifts as if a thought has come to her. Tugging at my shirtsleeve, she asks, "Were you here a couple of weeks ago? Some of my friends saw you on TV passing out rice and fishnets to villagers in Tan Lap. I told them it couldn't have been you since you'd let me know if you were in town."

My lips curl up in shame as the confession begrudgingly seeps out. I tell her how sorry I am for not contacting her sooner because of my hectic schedule. Expecting a lecture, I get a Mona Lisa smile instead. Before I know it, Grandmother shuffles me to the front of our ancestral altar, and in one dramatic sweep with her hands she says, "Now light an incense

Ngan Thuy Nguyen and her grandmother, Nguyen Thi Quyen. (Courtesy Ngan Thuy Nguyen)

and kneel." My ancestors approve of my charitable work, she says, which will add more "points" to our family fortune.

Grandmother offers me jasmine tea, and we sit quietly, sipping. The warmth of her presence contrasts dramatically with scenes of the last few weeks, and a solemn sorrow comes over me as I relive them.

AS WE'RE FLYING toward the somber evening lights of Saigon, I see from my window vast stretches of water shimmering against the shaded sunset. With my face pressed against the glass, I try to differentiate between rivers and land inundated by flood. The view from this height looks picturesque, almost serene, but my gut tells me that beneath the clouds lies unspeakable horror for the people of the Mekong Delta. No longer suffering from war, they're suffering from a different kind of struggle–fleeing from poverty and natural disasters. The two somehow always go hand in hand; one flood can wipe out twenty years of postwar development and destroy a family's livelihood and material possessions. I wipe my face with a steamy washcloth and let out a long sigh before closing my eyes. My mind is busy with images of devastation wreaked by a flood that observers are calling the worst in the Mekong Delta in seventy years.

It is the year of the golden dragon, and some believe that this dragon has unleashed its mystical torrential rage on the people and countryside of the delta. Who could not be afraid? I think about my own fears in the weeks before I boarded this plane to join my colleagues to assess the flood in our project areas. As early as August 2000 news of floods started trickling into the Oxfam office in Boston. Concern was focused on the early advent of the monsoon season, but at that point no one forecast the continuing downpour, lasting for three months. The stream of news flashes about flood refugees triggered unparalleled anxiety in me; these refugees could very well be my family in Vietnam. Images of Grandmother scooping floodwater from her house tormented me. I was afraid for her because I knew she was in great danger, like most inhabitants of the delta.

The burden of knowing too much about this familiar landscape and its people takes a toll on my mental state. My head starts to ache as I brace myself for our landing.

I AWAKE TO the distant cries of roosters, disoriented until I hear street hawkers hollering, "Banh Mi! Banh Mi!" Oh, yes, Saigon, and it is October. But where did the roosters come from? It's only 5:30 a.m., and the city is already coming to life, preparing for another day of relentless rain.

After spreading Laughing Cow processed cheese onto my piping hot banh mi–the omnipresent French bread and one of my favorite French legacies–I join my colleague, Tes Pilapil, in front of the guesthouse. A Land Cruiser pulls up and our colleagues from Can Tho University–Dr. Nguyen Van Be and Nguyen Thi Van Hong–step out. We cordially exchange greetings, and then the four of us set off on a flood assessment visit to the Plain of Reeds, starting with Long An province.

Two hours into the drive, we stop at a gas pump in the main town of Long An. From a distance I notice a sign that reads "Long An Hospital" gracing the side of a building. Dr. Be notices the wistful expression on my face. I hesitate before responding to his concern. Apprehensive about what local Vietnamese think about me, as a Viet Kieu–an overseas Vietnamese–I'm habitually cautious about information I give out about myself, fearing other people's judgment of me and my motives as a humanitarian worker. Pointing to the hospital, I turn to him and work up the courage to reveal that I was born here twenty-eight years ago.

His warm smile encourages me to divulge more unsolicited information. "I don't remember much about this place because I was so young when I left," I tell him. "But I've been back here enough times already to know it better."

"It's very courageous of you to visit and work in Vietnam," he says.

This statement, as simple and innocuous as it appears, can be interpreted in numerous ways. It can be construed as a political commentary: Am I courageous for working with a regime from which my family fled, a regime that will always mark me with suspicion? Or am I courageous for withstanding criticism from the overseas Vietnamese community for working with this regime? Perhaps each side sees a traitor in me–for leaving Vietnam, for returning to Vietnam. As a young Viet Kieu, I am a bridge to the future, helping to focus on Vietnam's economic and socio-political development.

Perhaps I am reading too much into Dr. Be's statement, finding implications where there are none. It's a strange sensitivity I have. I am, after all, not working for a regime but for the disadvantaged people of Vietnam. So long as my visits are for humanitarian purposes, I feel content about my complex relationship with this country.

Glancing again at the floodwater, I am conscious that the

word courageous should be attributed to the people coping with this disaster on a daily basis, not to me. Still, we all need protection, one way or another. Before Dr. Be or I can continue, our driver calls us back into the car where he lights incense and prays for a safe journey ahead.

We drive deeper into the province. Rice paddies that once graced the sides of the roads are submerged, and boats are a common sight. The main road that courses through Long An province is lined with flimsy, shabby tents sheltering thousands of flood victims. These makeshift tents stretch for miles on the horizon, crammed with families huddled together with their surviving livestock. I am not accustomed to seeing communities of tents in this part of the world. In my mind tents belong on recreational camping grounds or in a refugee camp in a conflict zone. They remind me of the ones in which my family resided when we were processed as political refugees after Saigon fell to Communist forces in 1975. Back then Mom made every effort to make our tent feel cozy. On one occasion she fed all five of us using one package of instant noodles she found in my bag. I was proud that my noodles saved us from hunger—for at least one afternoon. Mom would call us one by one to feed us the watery soup. Then Dad would enter the tent with three bottles of Coke, to a roar of cheers. I later learned that Dad had to barter his wristwatch to quench our thirst. He couldn't bear to see his children drool at the sight of other children's Cokes.

Now I have returned to the home of my ancestors again, after growing up in America and studying abroad, and each time I peer out the car window, I smile at the possibility that I might encounter a familiar face.

I first returned to Vietnam in 1992, after my mother's death. The reunion with Grandmother was poignant and hard; Mom was our link, and she was gone. With each succeeding visit since that first one, mostly for work, Vietnam became

In 2000 severe floods in the Mekong Delta of Vietnam displaced thousands of refugees. (Ngan Nguyen/Oxfam America)

more real to me. Chit-chatting under the mosquito netting, Grandmother became my teacher. We spoke of this land, its people, and its problems. Now here I am again, and as we drive past her flooded house, my heart nearly stops. I know she has been evacuated and is safe with a relative in a nearby town, but this does not shut down the anxieties. At 2.5 meters, the water is high enough to reach rooftops that were once the homes of our project beneficiaries. Along this route roads that we once traveled for monitoring visits are completely submerged. Indeed, the area is unrecognizable. I keep reminding myself that this is a farming and not a fishing community.

We board a rickety wooden boat. It is the only way to travel into Tan Lap, and though the water looks calm today, it may not be calm tomorrow if the rains continue. Even before we reach shore, a dozen or so women with warm and welcoming smiles wade through waist-deep water, grabbing our hands to lead us from the boat. How is it that these women are able to smile graciously in the face of disaster? Their smiles conceal hardship; stress lines on their faces reveal endless hours of worry and sleeplessness. There must be a story behind every wrinkle.

Ms. Nhan, the gaunt and humble vice-president of the district women's union, leads our small group through earthen dikes that shelter all 993 households in this village. "We still face starvation. We go for stretches without food," she says. "There have been times when we were so desperate we sought water hyacinths to eat at the risk of drowning."

She arches her conical hat to shield the sun's rays from my sunburned, flushed face. Unexpectedly, she sways her head next to mine and points at my face, whispering, "Too dark, like a peasant." A heroic smile materializes after she secures the hat on my head. I'm touched that despite all her worries, she is looking after me.

I look compassionately at the people we pass and start to feel self-conscious, even uncomfortable, recalling the eyes that looked upon us when we first arrived in a refugee camp in America. Every time we'd step forward to collect handouts, Dad would remind us to be gracious and to heed his warning: "Children, make sure you remember they're not pitying us, they're just helping us."

Our hosts offer us tea and dried instant noodles. "You must be hungry after the long trip. Please, have some," they say.

Vietnamese hospitality never ceases to move me. We accept and sip the tea, concealing our fear about the water's quality and source. Afterward, we take a brief tour. Each tent has an ancestral altar, sometimes the only possession saved from the floodwaters, a valuable asset not to be left behind. They are reminders of lineage. We are who we are because of our ancestors' deeds and are inextricably linked to them in the course of our life on earth. Mom used to say, "Go, bow to your ancestors and ask them to bless you," every time my siblings and I had to take exams. Of course, she made us study, too.

Families also have other needs: rice, water-purification tablets, a small boat, fishing gear. Tran Thi Cuc points to her wrecked boat: "We can't rely on handouts. None of the assistance lasts long. This is why we need boats and fishing gear—so that we can feed ourselves for months and prepare for the next big flood."

I listen carefully as Ms. Cuc describes the day when the water rose to dangerous levels, and she and her family had to flee. A neighbor banged on their door in the early hours of the morning, and all she could remember after that time was the desperation she felt holding on to as many of her five children as possible. She must have felt like Mom did when we had to evacuate Can Tho twenty-five years ago. I was irritated she gripped my hands so tightly as we dashed toward the helicopter.

"So, Ms. Ngan, where's your village?" Ms. Cuc asks, breaking my reverie. When I say, "Long An," a child screams out, "She's one of us!" I am encircled by warm embraces and bombarded with questions about the circumstances surrounding my departure from Vietnam and my life in America. Pressed for stories, I begin to describe my first trip back to Long An as a lone backpacker, which is a foreign concept here. Momentarily, one woman unleashes a sigh of disbelief and blurts: "I can't believe your father would allow his young daughter to travel across the world on her own. I'm not sure I'd even let my daughter go to the market by herself. He's a brave parent."

After the women in the group nod among themselves in agreement, the conversation soon returns to the flood and the refugees. Corpses have been covered with thin cloth and strapped to poles in positions above the water. Their grim presence no doubt generates unimaginable torment for their loved ones; until the flood recedes there can be no burial. Looking around, I'm reminded of Grandfather's stories about the horrors experienced by villagers in this area, who had to endure repeated attacks by the Khmer Rouge in the late 1970s. Captured villagers were gruesomely beheaded. Their heads were flaunted on stakes pierced in the ground for public viewing. It seems unfair that the cycle of suffering has returned.

Ten cups of tea later, we proceed toward our boat. After clumsily boarding, I turn around to acknowledge the children's farewell gestures. Their tiny hands wave wildly in the air. Some of the bolder ones edge toward the water, yelling, "Older sisters, don't forget us when you leave."

We promise to return.

FURTHER ALONG on our journey a community of roadside tents is abuzz with a makeshift clinic, café, and a hodgepodge of markets. People here seem to have adjusted to temporary life by carrying on with their business. We come across an awning made up of colorful collages of rice bags and discover a hair salon underneath. Women in curlers dangle their feet in the air while gossiping with their friends and barking at their mischievous children. We see money exchanged everywhere as we wander in this capitalist hub. Vietnamese people are renowned for their resilience in the face of disaster, resolutely living the motto "life goes on." This resilience has been inculcated in me, also, by Grandmother, most recently. She always says that one defining characteristic of the Vietnamese is that we can endure suffering of any depth and magnitude. We transcend hardship with an entrepreneurial and dignified spirit and, of course, a little cash.

After generous roadside portions of rice, fried fish with lemon grass and morning glory, we reach My Tho district in

Tien Giang province. It is already late afternoon. Every tree we pass looks dead–mango, guava, longan, banana. The view from Route 1–the country's national road linking north and south and the only road still standing in the province–resembles a vast sea drowning the fertile promises of the countryside. The only signs of life on either side are melaleuca trees. They appear stubbornly proud. Plastic tents pitched on the side of the road are reminiscent of Long An. In a review of major floods in this region over the past forty years–occurring in 1961, 1978, 1996, and 2000–the time intervals between these floods are getting shorter. We have meetings in which we discuss the prognosis for the future and immediate requirements. The construction of hundreds of wooden boats we want to distribute will take up to three weeks. I become agitated at the thought that, by the time the supplies arrive, they will provide only marginal relief.

HEAVY RAIN pounds our car. Warm and dry inside a guest house, I think again about the flood refugees who have scanty cover from the rain. The second I climb into bed, fatigue overwhelms me, then I'm wide awake. Images haunt me. In the dark I try to think happy thoughts, but recurring flashes of corpses suspended on poles and decapitated heads subvert these efforts. It's funny how the mind and eyes start playing tricks in the dark. I start to wonder if all the Vietnamese ghost stories my parents told us growing up are really true. My parents believed that where there's suffering and horrible death, there are also spirits that roam the land, confused and angry. My siblings and I couldn't get enough of these stories. Perhaps it was because we felt safe in the comfort of Louisiana, far from the land these ghosts frequented. Now they are here, all around me.

Tomorrow is October 31, my brother's birthday and also Halloween–an amazing coincidence on all counts. I fight back the thought of more ghosts. Candy. That's it! Halloween and candy go together. Then I think of Grandmother's candy factory in Long An and all the peanut brittle my teeth can handle for one afternoon. Drifting off, I see myself floating through Grandmother's factory as I eat autumn moon festival cakes, crystallized ginger, and Danish butter cookies. I sleep deliciously.

BY THE THIRD WEEK in November the grade school is reopened in Tan Lap and the village is returning to normal. Small clusters of women and children anxiously wait on shore as our group—consisting of me, Seth Amgott, an Oxfam colleague, and staff from Can Tho University and the Vietnam Women's Union—unpack the promised goods. "Blanket! Rice! Water system!" cries the village administrator as each woman, one by one, steps forward and nervously signs for her supplies. I run over to Ms. Cuc as soon as I see her approaching the freighter. We grab each other's hands, and she tells me, "I'm so grateful you saw us three weeks ago. I couldn't sleep last night, I was so excited." As she continues, her facial expression suddenly changes, "You know, Ms. Ngan, life will only get harder after the flood recedes, when we return to the nothingness of what used to be our homes."

I try to maintain my emotional composure and to be firmly optimistic for her. "Next time I visit, I hope to sip tea in your new home," I say.

A WOMAN with a deformed hand and a limp approaches me and asks for leftover supplies. I learn that her name is Moc The Hong. She lives in a neighboring village and is unable to receive relief because of our limited funds; we have targeted only the poorest in this geographical region. I feel so bad that the relief supplies aren't enough for people outside this village. I search around and locate a blanket and hand it to her. She seems happy with this but keeps pointing at my hair.

Another woman nearby laughs as she explains that Ms. Hong ekes out a living by plucking people's gray hairs, painlessly. Charging less than fifteen cents a head, she makes a dollar a day and manages to eat. Judging from the amount of gray hair on my head, she will be able to feed herself for an entire month. I obligingly bend down and become the focal point of entertainment for the children. As soon as Seth bursts into laughter, I point out gray hair on him and suggest that he could be the next customer.

With my head still throbbing from the tweezers' pull, I smile contentedly as I watch the women paddle away with their new boats and supplies. This is when the program officer becomes the beneficiary. Standing there, I feel proud of my chosen profession. Few understood why I wanted to go back to Vietnam in the early 1990s, at a time when Vietnam had few visitors and was still largely isolated.

As if he had read my mind, a TV journalist comes over and asks, "Why have you returned here?" Secretly, I want to scream out, "To tell all of you and your future generations that you're in danger–vulnerable to even more natural disasters." But I refrain and reply with professional optimism instead: "We assessed the flood situation three weeks ago and promised that we would be back with assistance. So, here we are today, taking part in helping this community bounce back."

He chuckles and adds, "That's good, but professional motives aside, what I really meant to ask was why did you choose to come back here to Long An when you left at such a young age?"

I am momentarily speechless. Questions float in my head: Was it a need to reunite with my family? Was it to whet my appetite for adventure? Was it the guilt I feel for having a better life? Or was it a deep caring for disadvantaged people I could identify with culturally? An ancestral grave barely above water behind the journalist's left shoulder prompts me to say the words that are flowing naturally from me: "My family's here, and my ancestors are here." I guess he's satisfied with my answer because, before I know it, he introduces me for the evening news as Ms. Ngan of Long An.

GRANDMOTHER REACHES over and offers me another plate of grilled bananas in coconut milk syrup. The red stains on her teeth glisten as she chortles at my overt and uninhibited affection toward her, which, she says, is "so American." But I know she's secretly tickled by such attention. There's nothing more special for me than to be able to cling to Grandmother's arm like an infant. I want to stay here, and I want her to protect me. Truth is, I also want to protect her. I know that her beloved home is a disaster-prone place with a future that could repeat past misfortunes. I resist another wave of temptation to lobby her to live with me in the United States, disinclined to put her in a position to reject my invitation yet again. It only dawned on me recently that every time I urge her to join me, she must be painfully reminded of a scene between her and my mother twenty-five years ago. When the South was crumbling to Communist forces, Mom tearfully begged Grandmother to escape with her and my father to the United States, but Grandmother agonizingly chose to stay behind, reminding her daughter between weeping to return as soon as it was safe. Tragically, that was the last time Grandmother saw her daughter, who never managed to return before her death.

Tomorrow I leave for Boston. Grandmother will summon me to the altar to ask for our ancestors' blessings, reminding me in her usual tone to be good because they'll always find me. In response, I'll say, "Are you telling me my ancestors have passports?" which never fails to elicit a roar of laughter from her. But this time I'll ask that our ancestors look after her in our homeland–the Mekong Delta–the birthplace of our ancestors.

4 *Invincible*
Chad

Christine Darcas

"As drought spread across the Sahara, I finally had the opportunity to roll up my sleeves and get into the field, to abandon my role as a bystander and make a difference."

There's a major boulevard in N'djamena that must have been beautiful once. Amid the gutted buildings and tarmac pocked by mortars, some peach archways have survived. They stand in the shade of trees, a pastel colonnade, lining each side like so many French roads. Relief workers who had been to Chad before the Libyan-backed civil war confirmed N'djamena's former beauty. Like Beirut used to be, they told me.

For a long time I wasn't scared when I drove down this avenue. Impressed, excited even, but not scared. I was in my mid-twenties and had already spent a year in N'djamena as a contractor with USAID, writing cables and reports, before I was drafted into its Food for Peace Office in 1985 to assist the US relief program in Chad. It was an assignment I wanted badly. I'd been interested in relief and development issues for several years and had majored in African studies and political science in college. I wanted to help, to do what I could to improve the livelihood of people in need. A summer working on an archeological dig in the Ivory Coast had already convinced me that I could live in—and explore—Africa indefinitely. I'd spend my career in development or relief work; I was sure of it. As drought spread across the Sahara, I finally had the opportunity to roll up my sleeves and get into the field, to abandon my role as a bystander and make a difference. Driving down that boulevard, weaving around the craters, I experienced the exhilaration of adventure and the certainty of my fortitude.

I was one of three members of the Food for Peace Office. Our work was varied. We monitored the use of American food aid to ensure it was being used and distributed as intended; reported on the famine's developments and the efforts by international relief agencies to alleviate it; lobbied for and procured additional funds from Washington for assistance that ranged from plastic sheeting for displaced persons' camps to manpower for food aid distributions. I traveled a lot, often for stints of two or three days. I always had a driver, usually Moussa, who drove over the sand for hours following only truck tracks to remote villages. Though golden desert stretched as far as the eye could see, we never got lost, and I never expected we would.

I checked warehouses, listening for weevils in food aid sacks and noting rodent droppings. I scanned the marketplace for potentially diverted food aid. I kept my ears open for word of unauthorized distributions. I visited supplementary feeding centers to confirm the numbers of frail, sunken children needing assistance. Many of them walked miles through sand and thick, hot air for their rations. They'd line walls made from mats, all of them holding their plastic mugs, waiting patiently. The sicker ones were taken to a different shelter where a doctor tended them.

At a woman's wail, I wheeled around to discover that her baby had just died. She cried and cried, and we were unable, truly helpless, to relieve her grief.

Following protocol, I visited the local officials before I roamed their villages. Over heavily sugared and minted tea, I'd hear their complaints, their pleas for more assistance. Though they spoke to me in French, they made side comments to assistants and servants in Chadian Arabic, a lan-

Christine Darcas, recovering from hepatitis in northern Cameroon, just over the border from Chad. (Courtesy Christine Darcas)

guage I depended upon Moussa to translate. Most officials treated me respectfully, but others were verbally aggressive. One official, a man rumored to have shot several men, slammed his hands on the table and shouted for more food.

USAID instructed relief workers dealing with American food aid to take military escorts when they traveled in the south. There was fighting there, skirmishes or village slaughters, depending on whom you believed. Some workers refused the escorts. If they were ambushed, better to show they were innocent helpers. To have an escort surely provoked a shootout. One of the Jesuit priests had been caught in an ambush and shot, someone said. He was fine. But that was just a rumor, maybe.

I usually flew into the south in a Cessna flown by two

French pilots. I traveled with members of other relief agencies, so I was never alone, though this didn't make any difference. I'd always loved to fly, to watch the ground drop away. Though I'd experienced turbulence during flights, it didn't bother me. One morning we took off in soft, easy sunshine. Clouds, scattered, then thick, closed in, surrounding us. The plane lurched and bounced through the sky. The pilots were scared. Though their smiles were reassuring, their shoulders were set with tension. A stream of water ran down the windshield. I focused on it, certain the water was seeping inside. At that moment, with the deepest terror, I believed the windshield would rupture, the plane disintegrate.

I collapsed when we landed in Sarh that day. I'd been in Chad for almost eighteen months by then. For the first time my legs betrayed me and gave way. From then on when I flew, I became nauseated. Pins and needles pricked my arms. I got hot, as though the airplane's thermostat were pushed up and nobody felt it but me.

The city of N'djamena, my home base, was supposedly safe, part of a secure zone between the hostile sections of the country. Though some fighting continued in the south, most of it was far away, north of the 16th parallel. The 16th parallel—as though a huge red line had been painted across the Sahara and the enemies had agreed to contain their battles on the other side. But even in N'djamena there were limitations on where I could go and what I could do. I was expected to follow rules: Don't go to the movie theater—a grenade could be thrown over the wall. The local "Westerner" nightclub, aptly called the Booby Bar and considered a terrorist target, was guarded by French soldiers until midnight. When they left, I was expected to leave too.

I traveled around the city on a third-hand moped. Colleagues cautioned me against purchasing it. A Médecins Sans Frontières (MSF) woman had been struck and killed by a truckload of combatants while riding a moped. Her body had been on the flight that had been bombed on the N'djamena runway months before. I ignored their advice. It couldn't happen to me.

I'd heard stories of shootouts among combatants in the city bars, bars filled with joyous, pulsing music that swept Chadians and expatriates onto the earthen floor. We danced in easy groups, reveling together in the musical strains. I was at such a bar one evening when a combatant approached me and ordered me to go outside with him. He hovered over me, his pistol at his side, reeking of alcohol. François-Xavier, an Action Internationale Contre la Faim (AICF) representative I'd seen at several meetings, urged me not to make eye contact. "Ne le regardes pas," he said. Drinking his beer and sitting calmly next to me, he repeated it quietly until the soldier turned and left. I thanked him. He shrugged. It was no big deal.

Most of my friends were stationed in the field away from the city. In N'djamena I'd drive my moped home past knobby-kneed children in grayed, torn clothes, past one-room "cases" built from "banco," a mixture of straw and dried mud, past traffic signs riddled with bullet holes. In the streets children's voices were everywhere, a constant, melodic chatter.

I hardly heard them in my compound. An arid stillness filled my house, punctured only by a woman pounding sorghum or the squawking of chickens. Perhaps that's why I went to the Booby Bar that Saturday night and stayed there after midnight. There were big meetings in town that week; many of the agencies had pulled their workers in from the field. They were there, kids, like me. We drank and danced until the gunshots rang out and the music stopped cold. For an instant, we stared at each other, restraining panic, wondering if the shots were real, before we hit the ground. French off-duty soldiers apprehended the gunman quickly, and we were soon free to return home.

I walked down the street amid fourteen-year-olds with AK-47s slung over their shoulders. They hadn't bothered me much, but I started keeping my distance. I imagined a boy dropping his weapon, it going off, hitting me.

One morning I turned on the BBC to discover that the Americans had bombed Tripoli and Benghazi, major cities in Libya, directly north of Chad. I stayed at my kitchen table, glued to reports speculating that Qaddafi hadn't survived, that some of his family were dead. I understood then that we—Americans in Chad—had become potential targets, marks for revenge. Perhaps we had been all along, but I hadn't felt it until that moment. It wouldn't take much to pick one of us off. We were advised to vary our routes, to stay alert, as if it could make a difference.

I saw more of François when possible. He spent a lot of time in the field working on irrigation projects, sometimes weeks on end. One day a young Chadian arrived at my office to tell me François was sick with malaria. I wasn't immediately concerned; malaria and recurrent cases of it were relatively common among the agency reps. As long as the person was basically healthy, he or she muddled through. But when a day went by with no word from François, I went to the radio and tried to raise him. He didn't respond. A Chadian, his voice anxious, got on to say that François was too ill to speak. He was in Doba, far in the south, a couple of days away by car.

We'd started readying a plane when we received word over the radio that the local Catholic mission had stepped in to care for François. He returned several days later, gaunt, still carrying the acrid smell of fever. He'd lost at least four kilos. He'd started to recover after the Catholic mission had given him a shot of Fanzidar. It was pure luck that he'd been near a place that had the medicine. Once again, he shrugged. As sick as he'd been, he hadn't believed he could die.

There were quiet times and easier moments. I made a

couple of trips down south after the rains returned and drove by fields tall with red sorghum. The trees were lush green, so different from the brush and sand of N'djamena or the sweeping desert of the far north. I swam in the Logone River, sat on mats, drank beer, and chatted with locals. Children approached me, touched my skirt, giggled, and ran away. Even in N'djamena there were times when I relaxed this way. There, at sunset, I listened as the call for prayer rolled over the city from the mosque. In those moments I forgot about the work, the poverty, the sick children, the children with guns, the civil viciousness.

I started losing weight. Between the famine and destruction, the quantity and range of food in N'djamena were limited. Business was just creeping back into the city. There were a few restaurants, small stores selling canned goods and soap, but no supermarkets carrying chips and chocolates. I didn't think much about food preparation anyway. After a while I stopped eating red meat. I couldn't stomach it. Sometimes my gut would spasm. I ignored it, assumed it was nothing. On the weekends I slept until 1 p.m. I dragged myself out of bed during the week to work. I forced myself to move, to find some energy to get through the day.

I went on home-leave for three weeks. At the N'djamena airport soldiers searched the passengers and checked all the luggage. They looked for bombs slipped on the plane at the beginning of its route in Bangui. One plane had already made an emergency landing in Algiers because of a bomb threat. Flying to Paris, I worried that I'd be blown out of the sky.

I didn't do much at home. It was cold. I slept, wandered shops for clothes, nonperishable foods, tapes, sheets—supplies I couldn't find in Chad. I wanted to visit friends but didn't have the energy. I complained to my doctor about my stomach spasms and lethargy. He sent me for X-rays and gave me a standard blood test, but he didn't find anything abnormal.

*In 1984, refugees in Chad flee drought-stricken areas for the town of N'djamena.
(UN Photo 154290/John Isaac)*

I asked him if I should be tested for parasites, but he seemed uncertain how to even go about it. When I suggested hepatitis, he shook his head. "If you had hepatitis," he said, ushering me out of his office, "you'd know it."

I returned to Chad. Within two weeks I started throwing up everything I ate. A colleague stopped me one morning and asked if I'd looked in the mirror. "Look at your eyes," he said. I went to the bathroom to stare at whites that had turned yellow. I weighed ninety-eight pounds, a weight I hadn't seen since I was twelve years old.

I stayed in Chad for my recovery from hepatitis. Though weak, I could walk, talk, and care for myself. One afternoon Moussa came by. His brow was furrowed and he tsk-tsked at the sight of me. I'd grown too thin, he said. His wife could make me a mixture, a brew. It had helped him.

It wouldn't be until years later that I'd fully appreciate how much Moussa had taken care of me in the field: He'd stocked the Land Cruiser, found us food and lodging, translated for me, always known where I was. He struggled to provide for his own family, yet he reached out to help me. I did not take his brew. I wish I had.

Within a month I was back in the field. My first time out was a plane trip to Mao with a World Food Program (WFP) representative. We'd hardly been there a couple hours before I felt weak again. I excused myself to lie on a couch in the compound. Lying there, I stared out the window at sand. It seemed to be everywhere in Mao—on the windowpanes, the floor, in my hair and clothes. At that moment I wanted more than anything to be in my own bed, to escape that place and find the peace of sleep.

Hostilities resurged in the north, and the French military returned in earnest. By then, François and I were living together in a house about a mile from the airport. We listened all night to the drone of military planes flying in. But early one morning, another plane, faster, screamed in under the others.

The explosion shook the house. Dirt flew against the low vent in my bathroom wall. I tore out of bed. François had only just left. I didn't know where he was, whether he had been close to the explosion or not. Perhaps it was a bomb, the first of many, the beginning of an onslaught. Maybe a plane had crashed. I stood in the yard, uncertain whether to hide or search for him. Within minutes a voice on my embassy radio announced that a Libyan plane had dropped a bomb at the airport. It fell right outside the control tower and missed the runway.

Startled chickens, that's all, had sprayed the dirt against my wall. Yet it had felt so close. François called me from his office. Driving, he had seen people running for cover but hadn't heard the bomb.

For what seemed like weeks afterward, French fighter planes—les mirages—roared into the airport in the early morning hours. As I took my shower, their engines whistled through the bathroom tiles. I turned off the water and listened, anticipating the shift in sound to the bomber's scream.

A few months later, as my contract neared completion, my boss asked me if I wanted to stay on. I refused. Whatever drive, whatever commitment, I'd felt two years before had disappeared. Try as I might, I couldn't summon it back. I wanted to leave, to return home where life was predictable and safe. François, however, wanted to stay. Though Chad had left me with a rattled sense of mortality, he remained unflappable. In roughly the same two-year period, François had discovered that he could stick with it and I'd discovered that I couldn't.

In the first of what would be many concessions between us, François agreed to come to the United States. We moved to a small apartment in Philadelphia and married. He was interested in getting his MBA. While he did business-school applications, I slept, read, took a few business courses, and generally procrastinated about my professional future. I was lost, didn't know anymore what I wanted to become, what to aim for. I'd abandoned one path and couldn't find another.

I finally focused on finding work that involved analytical and organizational skills, skills I was sure I wanted to continue using. I interviewed for a few jobs before it became clear that I needed an MBA to make that transition, given my background. The interviewers regarded my experience with curiosity. On the one hand, it seemed impressive, courageous even, they said. On the other, it was unconventional. They expressed concern about my suitability for corporate life. They questioned my motivation. Why would I ever want to go to Chad? Their perplexity frustrated me. Why wouldn't I? Why wouldn't

Rural farmers in Chad plant millet. (UN/Carl Purcell)

they want to explore people, cultures, and issues beyond their own? In people I met, I equated international disinterest with self-absorption, consumerism with petty superficiality—presumptions that weren't always fair, I realized.

Several years later I was snug and safe at my desk in New York City when I read about the plane exploding between N'djamena and Paris, killing Peace Corps volunteers. It had happened to them. Sitting there, staring at the newspaper, I thought how none of them would have really believed they could die when they signed on. Perhaps they were told Chad was dangerous, just as I had been told. But conscious as I was of the risks in my early days, I hadn't felt them. Feeling them made all the difference.

An armed gang in Sierra Leone. (David Snyder)

Part Two

War

When I began this project, I did not expect that most of the stories would take place in conflict zones. As a child of refugees, I resisted this sad reality for a long time, until I could resist it no longer. The war stories came in at an unrelenting pace. As I write, almost one in five of the 191 nations in the world is at war—declared or undeclared—with another nation or within its own borders. In 2001 and 2002, 40 percent of all wars were being fought in Africa. But there were also renewed border clashes in Korea and Kashmir, suicide bombings in Israel, intensified Israeli military occupation in Palestine, an attack on the World Trade Center in New York, the bombing of Afghanistan, continuing war in Chechnya, internecine fighting in Colombia. Wars end, new ones begin. Most, but not all, take place in underdeveloped states, often former colonies, or former client-states, of richer first-world nations.

History is a poor teacher, and it is also—paradoxically—the best of teachers. The lesson of brutality, even of hacked-off limbs, has been taught well; it was a Belgian specialty in the Congo during the 1890s European "scramble for Africa." King Leopold II claimed humanitarian action as his motivation—saving the "natives" from the Afro-Arab slave trade, converting the barbarians to Christianity. This was a cynical deception; what a shock to see the word humanitarian in his writings. The Belgian genocide in the Congo stirred the first human rights campaign in modern history, most of which was heartfelt, some of which was hypocritically righteous; the crimes against humanity of the other colonial powers were also egregious, though often unreported.

That was a mere three generations ago, and there is violence again, or still, in Congo, and all around the globe. What has emerged in recent years is frightening: grotesque brutality, murder of genocidal proportions, the collapse of civil order, of civilization itself. The International Criminal Court will never be idle.

How do humanitarian workers cope in such difficult and dangerous circumstances? They do not carry guns, they are not diplomats. It is not their mandate, in fact, to resolve the political, postcolonial, or post–Cold War conundrums. Their task is modest, marginal, sometimes inflammatory, though this is never intentional. The food they distribute may be used to feed soldiers instead of victims, thus perpetuating the conflict. Or medical supplies may be stolen and find their way onto the black market. Humanitarian workers may be perceived as partisan and held hostage, or raped, and killed. Even worse, perhaps, their presence on the ground may be used as an excuse for political and diplomatic inaction, thus prolonging a war for years, as happened in Bosnia. As gunfire escalates, they are evacuated quickly, or they are caught in a crossfire and cannot be evacuated, or they decide to stay and help whatever victims they can, putting their own lives at risk. Just as it is impossible to prevent terrorism entirely, humanitarian workers cannot be fully protected in the field. Still, one wonders if they are protected enough, and what more can be done by the international community that funds their work.

5 *Surviving Genocide*
Rwanda

Philippe Gaillard

"But we did not turn tail; in the hell of Kigali, we talked to all the devils. Nor did we abandon our Rwandan staff or the people of Rwanda."

On April 6, 1994, at around eight o'clock in the evening, a plane carrying Rwandan President Juvénal Habyarimana and Burundan President Cyprien Ntaryamira was shot down by missile fire over Kigali airport. At that moment I was in a meeting with leaders of the Rwandan Patriotic Front (RPF) inside the Parliament building. The Parliament had been rebel headquarters since the previous December, after a "peace agreement" between the Hutu government and the Tutsi rebels had been signed in Arusha, Tanzania, in August 1993. The building itself was situated on the outskirts of Kigali, and as soon as the assassination was announced on the radio, government troops gathered and began shooting bullets and mortars.

Two of my International Committee of the Red Cross (ICRC) colleagues, Hervé Le Guillouzic, medical doctor, and Marco van Inthoudt, relief coordinator, were with me. We spent the night at the back of a room flooded with water, surrounded by sandbags. We could not sleep. We were silent. So were the RPF leaders. We wondered what was to come the next day. After fourteen years in the field, I had never before been in such an acute situation.

The systematic massacres began on the morning of April 7. Although they took place hundreds of meters away, we could see—through the huge windows of the Parliament—that people were being chased and slaughtered. We were trapped with RPF soldiers inside the Parliament. They seethed with rage and impatience as they helplessly watched the killings take place and argued furiously with the few UN military representatives there, begging them to intervene or to let them, the RPF fighters, intervene. But there was no swaying the UN soldiers, probably because of their mandate; they were there to keep the fragile peace, not to intervene in a battle. Everybody seemed lost and desperate.

The tension mounted. I was being pressed by my two colleagues to leave the building. They, in turn, were under intense pressure from their wives, who were constantly calling from their homes in Kigali. Fortunately, my wife, Maria Teresa, also an ICRC delegate, had left Rwanda for holiday with her family in Colombia ten days earlier, so I could fully concentrate.

Staying in the Parliament building with the RPF meant being a military target; leaving meant exposing ourselves to the bullets, the roadblocks, and the wrath of God. We finally decided to go, followed by the voices of the RPF members and the UN officers, both calling us reckless idiots.

It was just before noon. We easily reached my vehicle, which was parked outside. It was a small Japanese car with a Red Cross insignia. Before joining their wives and children, I told my colleagues that we would first pick up our secretary, Muriel, who had stayed behind alone in one of our houses. When we arrived ten long minutes later, her neighborhood was motionless, as if everybody had fled or was hiding behind closed doors. I rang the bell, and she opened the door.

"Just take your passport and a couple of clothes, Muriel. We will leave your home within five minutes," I said.

I hastily informed her about the assassination of President Habyarimana and the slaughter that had started. She was afraid and relieved that we had picked her up.

Philippe Gaillard talking to Colonel François Munyengango, liaison officer of the Rwandan Armed Forces to the International Committee of the Red Cross. The colonel, who died of AIDS in 1994, saved 600 orphans in Butare during the genocide. Behind them stands Jean-Pascal Chapatte, administrator of the ICRC delegation. (Courtesy Philippe Gaillard)

The next step was to reach the homes of my two colleagues. On the way, at one roadblock, drunken government soldiers stopped us, demanding our car. I got out and introduced myself to their commander, who was especially drunk. I shook his hand and asked his name.

"I will not tell you," was his reply.

At times like this the most important thing is not to show how scared you are, to keep cool, look people straight in the eye and, even if it means telling the odd fib, that is OK. You cannot learn to come up with convincing arguments; it's a matter of intuition, a tool of survival. As Céline wrote in his *Journey to the End of the Night,* "On the brink of being drawn and quartered, some minds are capable of extraordinary feats of imagination!"

Without batting an eyelid, I told the drunken officer a lie: I was a neighbor of the minister of defense, Augustin Bizimana, and of the chief of cabinet of his ministry, Colonel Téoneste Bagosora, and I would most certainly inform them of the undisciplined behavior encountered at this roadblock.

The soldier appeared to be moved by my familiarity with the hierarchy and let us pass. Two minutes earlier, his machine gun had been pointed at my stomach. I could not believe that my imagination had saved us.

As we came to my colleagues' homes, I saw militiamen in the streets with machetes, screwdrivers, and hand grenades. No imagination at this moment was necessary to realize what was happening: Rwanda had become a giant execution chamber, something that probably had no precedent since the Second World War, with the exception of Pol Pot's Cambodia. No wonder all the UN agencies, all the NGOs, and all the development and cooperation projects had bolted their doors and left the country. France had sent paratroopers to evacuate expatriates only; others had gone by road, leaving behind their desperate Rwandan staff. By April 21, the twenty-five hundred UN troops were reduced to four hundred, leaving the courageous General Romeo Dallaire, head of the UN peacekeeping force, badly off indeed. The UN Assistance Mission for Rwanda (UNAMIR) had become a political and logistical phantom.

WE DECIDED to assemble all of the ICRC staff at the delegation, which was located close to the center of the town and the main governmental institutions–the Ministry of Defense and the headquarters of the Rwandan Armed Forces. We also decided to evacuate the expatriate wives, their children, and those delegates who weren't absolutely essential.

With the help of the Rwandan Red Cross, we also started to take injured people to a school a few feet away from the delegation, which we had transformed into a field hospital.

We were aware—though probably not all of us to the same extent—that caring for the victims of such a violent situation was a futile gesture. The violence gripping Rwanda was not designed to neutralize the enemy by taking him prisoner or wounding him but purely and simply to eliminate him.

The days passed, and we steadfastly continued our work. I met with various interlocutors—both from the government and the RPF. I monitored the political and military evolution of the situation and shared analysis and information with General Dallaire and my headquarters in Geneva. I managed and supported the delegation staff members as they operated on the wounded in our makeshift hospital. These wounded had not been finished off by the machetes and the screwdrivers, they were still alive, but barely. I gave interviews to whatever reporters were still in the country.

Twice, our ambulances were stopped by militia roadblocks. Both times the wounded were forcibly unloaded and murdered before our eyes. Radio-TV Libre des Mille Collines announced that the ICRC was transporting, and I quote, "enemies of the Republic disguised as injured people." Subsequent protests, explanations, and press releases from Geneva were taken up by the media. This did have a positive effect on the ground, as the Rwandan government suddenly realized the extent of the damage to its image. It then launched an awareness-raising campaign regarding the rights of the wounded to medical care, and the role of the Red Cross.

I guess we had gone through some kind of test. We could have been killed for making our statements to the international media regarding the massacre, but we were not. As a result of this exposure, the Red Cross ambulances were able to continue their work without hindrance. Between April 10 and July 4, the height of the genocide, we managed to take care of nine thousand wounded in our makeshift hospital.

In a conflict that killed almost a million people in less than three months, nine thousand, I suppose, is just a drop of humanity in an ocean of blood. Was it worth the risks we took to save this drop of humanity? Today it is easy to say yes, but at the time the answer was not obvious at all. Most of us, local staff and expatriates, were in our thirties, full of energy, and really in love with life. Some ICRC delegates became sick with doubt, others were psychologically affected. Out of over thirty expatriates, only three were able to get through this experience unscathed. All the others were replaced by new voluntary staff.

It was a season in hell, an obscene and ferocious madness. Hundreds of people were fleeing Kigali, fleeing the countryside, as the RPF gained ground. But we did not turn tail; in the hell of Kigali, we talked to all the devils. Nor did we abandon our Rwandan staff or the people of Rwanda.

The prefecture of Kigali needed petrol to collect corpses in dump trucks, so we gave them some. An official in the prefecture told us three weeks later that they had evacuated sixty-seven thousand corpses in the city of Kigali alone. For lack of chlorine and aluminum sulphate, Kigali found itself without water. We brought in the chemicals needed, thereby postponing, by two weeks, the death throes of the central pump works.

Toward the middle of April the interim government fled Kigali and went south to Gitarama. It was sad indeed to see all these ministers leaving the Hôtel des Diplomates in downtown Kigali, carrying their own bags, with their kids in tears. One of them was out of petrol, so I gave him some. Another one had no car and asked me to help him. I put him in the car of the one to whom I had just given fuel. The hotel was now almost emptied of its august and noble occupants. It was pathetic. I didn't know whether to laugh or cry.

What in my life had ever prepared me for such a moment? Strong skepticism, on the one hand, and, on the other, poetry. And poetry, a great enthusiasm since I was a teenager, helped me through this reign of terror. The strength

United Nations medical soldiers attend to a child wounded by a landmine outside the Central Hospital of Kigali. (UNICEF/94-0454/Betty Press)

of the poetic images gave me solace during those hard days in Rwanda. I read aloud, for myself, but mostly for my colleagues, especially before dinner. It was a kind of prayer, a kind of sanity, a grounding. I still remember these words of Rimbaud: "Through what crime, by what fault did I deserve my present weakness? You who imagine that animals sob with sorrow, that the sick despair, that the dead have bad dreams, try now to relate my fall and my sleep. I can explain myself no better than the beggar with his endless Aves and Pater Nosters. I no longer know how to talk."

My voice broke as I read this passage to my silent colleagues.

That evening, after the evacuation of the interim government from Kigali to Gitarama, I drank a fair bit of alcohol. Our administrator, Jean-Pascal, had managed to buy some 1986 Pauilhac for five dollars a bottle on the black market. All the luxury shops and ambassadors' residences had been looted by then, and this is probably where the bottles came from. Later, in my sleep, I dreamed that I wasn't in Kigali; I was alone in a Cistercian monastery in the middle of New York, and the monastery was on fire. It was magnificent.

A few days later we set up a subdelegation in Gitarama or, more accurately, in Kabgayi, the bastion of Catholicism in the country, about fifty kilometers south of Kigali. Kabgayi had a hospital and many other places where almost thirty-five thousand civilians, most of them Tutsi, had taken refuge, each of them vulnerable to the fury of the Hutu militiamen. Hundreds of them were massacred during targeted, expertly organized night raids. The bishops were there too, but they kept quiet. Later on, in June, the bishops themselves were killed in a mad rage by young rebels of the RPF.

There were massive problems in finding ways to protect these people. Several times I went from Kigali to Kabgayi to talk to the religious and government authorities, to remind them of their responsibilities, and to bring their ministers and military officers to the scene so that they could see for themselves the scale of the disaster and the subhuman conditions their people were living in, irrespective of their ethnicity.

They agreed, but their disorganization, the military advance of the rebels, and the prospect of losing the war, combined with their overwhelming feeling of powerlessness were such that, ultimately, they were unable to put an end to the murderous madness and systematic massacre that most of them had organized. There were those whose feelings were so anesthetized that they could not respond at all, or could respond only with indifference or despair. Once, when I asked Jacques Bihozagara, a high-ranking dignitary of the RPF who later became a minister and then an ambassador, whether he knew what was happening, he said to me, "Mr. Gaillard, we know perfectly what is going on, but we also know that, even after Hiroshima, there were survivors."

His words have remained carved in my head, like transparent ice in a crack that has split one rock into two.

Later on, we came to learn that the machetes and screwdrivers used during the Rwandan genocide killed at least seven times more people than the Hiroshima nuclear bomb.

Still, I must say this: I also met, among the Hutu government officials, clear-headed people who saved lives. Not all of them behaved like monsters. As in WWII in Europe, there were also some righteous people in Rwanda in 1994.

I am thinking especially of Colonel François Munyengango, who had been, at our request, appointed military liaison officer with the ICRC delegation by the minister of defense himself. Colonel François was in the terminal phase of AIDS and, perhaps because of that, took incredible risks in helping us to save hundreds of defenseless civilians, including six hundred orphans in the southern city of Butare.

I am thinking, too, of some of the authorities in the Cyangugu prefecture who, in spite of the immense military pressure on them, did everything possible to prevent the murder of the eight thousand civilians placed in the Nyarushishi camp, the only Tutsi survivors in the whole of Cyangugu.

THE RPF'S MILITARY advance was impressive. By the end of May the rebels had taken Byumba, Kayanza, and Rwamagana. They controlled the Tanzanian border. They had crossed the Bugesera and cut off the road leading from Kigali to the border with Burundi, a little to the north of

Butare. A few days later Kabgayi and Gitarama fell into the hands of the rebels. In Kabgayi the ICRC delegates emerged unscathed, as did the wounded soldiers of the government army who were in our hospital and hadn't been able to flee with the rest of their troop.

The rebels forced the ICRC workers to leave Kabgayi, which was thought to be too dangerous. Through satellite phone from Kigali, I ordered my colleagues to submit to the commands of the RPF. They were then moved to Nyanza with all the war-wounded. The wounded soldiers from the government army were fortunately regarded by the RPF as prisoners of war. And over thirty thousand civilians, most of them Tutsi, who had taken refuge in Kabgayi and who had spent almost two months in a living nightmare, were alive. Considering the situation, this was a miracle.

In the meantime the ICRC had opened a subdelegation in Ngara, Tanzania, to help around 300,000 refugees who had fled the advance of the RPF. Among these refugees were numerous militiamen whose hands were undoubtedly covered with blood. My colleagues over there were perplexed by this. I told them we were not a court of justice. Within twelve hours they had distributed four-day food rations to each family of refugees. I don't regret any of it; a child should not starve because his or her father is a criminal.

Whereas one month before we had been wondering whether or not to leave Rwanda, now the ICRC had a presence in six different places in the country, in both the government-held and the rebel-held areas.

In Kigali itself our situation was still uncomfortable. In mid-May one of our food convoys was deliberately targeted by the RPF while leaving Kigali for Gitarama. For one and a half hours, three ICRC delegates–Pierre Gratzl, François Conrad, and Ian Stefanski–were caught in a hail of bullets and mortars. Pierre Gratzl was wounded in the abdomen by an exploding shell. General Dallaire from the UNAMIR was able to rescue him with two armored cars. Pierre was operated on in our hospital, and that day I learned a new word: laparotomy—quite a touchy medical operation on the inside of the body to make sure that no shrapnel has been left behind.

Pierre is a school friend; we have known each other for almost thirty years. I am pretty sure—even though it is hard to say this when you are as shy as I am—that he would not have agreed to come to Rwanda if I had not been there myself, and I felt responsible. I called his mother in Switzerland to explain that Pierre had been injured but was out of danger.

When death, with its many odors, is constantly on the prowl, washing is important. My stomach is as regular as clockwork. Hell outside, order inside. So I went to the toilet every morning as soon as I got up. When I took a shower, I collected the water in a plastic bucket. Kigali's water supply had stopped in May, and we were retrieving water from a local stream. Sometimes I would cry, crouched down in the bathtub. My tears mingled divinely well with the water. Then I poured all this dirty water into the toilet, flushing away my excrement into the city's sewers.

These technical details are important now. How did we survive? The truth has far more to do with psychiatry than home economics. The fact is that, under such circumstances, it is essential for one's own mental balance to be able to get rid of one's own shit with one's own tears. The pH of the whole body, and of the soul as well, then returns to normal. The night's acidity disappears and one can walk again, without stumbling.

The day after my boyhood friend's surgery on the bullet wound to his stomach, I was walking again, without stumbling.

One week later a mortar fell on the ICRC delegation, instantly killing two people and wounding five others. Fortunately, I was in town at that time. I immediately returned to my office; it was upside down, full of dust, with a hole in the wall. This was too much. The mortars had come once again from the RPF! At the very start of the conflict, in October 1990, the RPF had given us categorical assurances that it would respect international humanitarian law, the ICRC mandate, and the work of the delegates. Contact between the ICRC and the rebel movement was regular and known to everyone, including the Rwandan government. Had the RPF's attitude toward us changed? To find out, we had to meet the rebels, if possible, at the highest level.

It was the ICRC's head of operations for Africa, Jean-Daniel Tauxe, who traveled from Geneva to Uganda. For my part, I took advantage of the fact that my friend General Dallaire and the UN High Commissioner for Human Rights, Ambassador José Ayala Lasso, were heading toward the north of the country, and I went by road to Byumba. There I met General Paul Kagamé, the rebel leader, and requested a meeting for Jean-Daniel Tauxe and myself for two days later. This was immediately granted by General Kagamé.

When I told him about the RPF bombing on our premises, General Kagamé said to us, "It's not our intention to shoot you."

"General, it is good to know that, but please don't kill us, even by mistake," I said.

Then we laughed. It is a comfort to learn that if you have to die, it will be by mistake!

OUR MAKESHIFT HOSPITAL was becoming seriously overcrowded. I decided to transfer patients from our hospital in the government-held zone to the King Faisal Hospital in the RPF-held zone. The King Faisal Hospital was full of dirty papers and other detritus. A logistics expert from the Canadian Red Cross managed to create a clear area in the hospital, which was then serving as a camp for thousands of people. Within a couple of days, 100 beds, a couple of wards,

In 1994, these Rwandan children lost their parents in a massacre. Here they rest at Ndhosha camp in Goma, Zaire. (UN Photo 186797/J. Isaac)

and one operating theater were ready. Those patients considered fit to travel, both Hutu and Tutsi, were put on the back of a lorry. I led the first convoy. The journey entailed crossing a bridge that spanned a valley. The bridge was an exposed and terrifying place to be. A couple of days earlier a UN peacekeeper had been killed there by an RPF mortar. But we went through and repeated the cross-line operation many times.

At the end of June one of the convoys of mainly Tutsi wounded was stopped on the bridge by presidential guards. I argued in vain as one of them climbed into the back of the lorry to "inspect the wounded." A crowd of Hutu gathered and started shouting "cockroaches," the most malicious word to call a Tutsi. Some brandished machetes. I jumped into my car, drove like a madman to the barracks of the chief of staff of the governmental army, got a handwritten piece of paper with a stamp, and then drove back to the bridge and showed the guard the paper. I watched nervously while the guard radioed headquarters and was told to let the lorry through. The convoy moved off. When it reached the other side, there was an RPF roadblock. The commander there also insisted on "inspecting the wounded." Among them in the back of the lorry the commander found his brother. "You have brought my brother back! You have brought my brother back," he cried.

AT THE END OF JUNE, the RPF made a "mistake" again. When two shells fell right on top of the emergency ward of our hospital, killing seven patients and wounding a dozen others, I was beside myself.

I alerted the BBC, CNN, Radio France Internationale, and the rest of the media to tell them of our woes, thinking this would be one way of teaching the RPF artillerymen better aim. Though typically addicted to fast-food news, the international press does have its good side; news gets out quickly. The RPF knew this and did not like seeing its image as a disciplined, organized army respectful of the Geneva Conventions being eroded in this way.

Between the end of June and the very start of July, Alexis Kanyarengwe, the president of the RPF, sent us two letters asking us to move our delegation and our hospital to another part of Kigali. I definitely prefer receiving letters to artillery shells. Kigali was surrounded by the rebels, and it would not be long before it fell.

On July 2, three months after the massacres began, six drunken Hutu militiamen with machetes and machine guns came to our hospital. They brought with them a Tutsi nurse.

"We are leaving the town," one said. "We decided not to kill her despite the fact that she is a Tutsi. We think she will be more useful in your hospital than dead. Thank you for what you have been doing here."

By dawn on July 4 the RPF troops were circulating freely throughout the city of Kigali. I dined once more with General Dallaire, who presented me with a ribbon. As a present, I gave him my Red Cross badge, reminding him that he was not entitled to wear it. Although our mandates were very different, General Dallaire had lived through the same nightmare as I, and maybe worse; he had lost thirteen of his men, ten of them in appalling circumstances—shot at pointblank range—and a price had been put on his head by the Hutu militias. Since the beginning of June, General Dallaire had not been able to cross the front lines and was living as a recluse in his headquarters.

All through the genocide I had been in contact with my wife by phone. At the end of April she returned to the northern part of Rwanda which was under full control of the RPF, and therefore rather safe. She worked there distributing food to the civilian population, and we were then in regular contact by radio. She never put any pressure on me to leave the country. We met again in the southern town of Kabale on July 6, 1994, my birthday, and the day I left Rwanda forever.

I was lucky. We were lucky. Only three of our Rwandan staff were killed. All of their close relatives were saved. Their children, dozens of them, used to hide in the corridors of the delegation when there was shelling. I played with them any time I could. Eventually, they began to call me "Grandfather."

6 *My Bodyguard*
Somalia

Patrick Dillon

"How to describe the next six months? Pornographic is the only English word that comes close. Soft-core, not the hard stuff, at least not until the end. That was a snuff film."

He was my bodyguard. He had big brown eyes, a quick white grin, a Kalashnikov knock-off with a bayonet fixed to its business end, sharp enough to shave with. His name was Muhammad Ali, just like the Champ, and he was ten years old. That's not a misprint, dear reader, you got it right the first time. My bodyguard, *he was ten*.

I met him the morning I arrived in Huddur, in 1992, just after dawn. Huddur was the Somali desert backwater some fifty-odd clicks from the Kenya border where I was to finish building a makeshift refugee camp consisting of a dirt airstrip and a sprawling circuit of feeding centers. It was a race against time, a desperate attempt to save the lives of some fifty thousand sick and starving tribes people, Nomads, who'd fled in terror from the burned-out bush country to the north and west, who'd been turned back from the border repeatedly by Kenyan Army Ranger sharpshooters with standing orders to shoot them on sight, and who'd coalesced in and around Huddur by dint of rumors of food and fresh water.

My job was to complete the work begun by Sean Lee, a pug-nosed, barrel-chested Irish policeman and ex-I.R.A. hunter who worked for Concern Worldwide, an Irish relief agency. Concern had just been contracted by the UN to

Muhammad Ali, Patrick Dillon's bodyguard. (Patrick Dillon)

become its official NGO in charge of food distribution in Somalia.

Sean Lee filled me in on some of Somalia's sordid little colonial history while we drove. Did I know, for instance, that in 1968 Henry Kissinger himself installed the dictator, Said Barre, and after a speech in Mogadishu, Herr Doktor K signed a security agreement that would reap Barre and his blood-soaked regime a cool $100 million *per year,* in cash and military hardware, to guard the Horn, the Gulf of Hormuz, for the next twenty years. Out of the Horn flowed 70 percent of the world's oil. Did I know about *that,* Yank? When he finished his history lesson, Sean Lee slapped me on the shoulder, laughed, shook his fist at the sky, and we roared off through a brown tunnel of heat and dust toward Huddur proper. We were meeting with the leaders of the various clans assembled there and awaiting word on when or whether anything more than rumor would begin flowing into the feeding centers. Their people were dying in droves, not from starvation so much as from disease, and Sean then informed me we were right in the middle of a measles outbreak that had already killed over four hundred babies in less than two days. It would kill more than another four hundred in the next twenty-four hours, and I would be left to bury the babies, passels of them, without shrouds, a sacrilege, according to the Qur'an.

HUDDUR, MY NEW HOME, emerged millennia ago as an inland oasis, a crossroads bazaar situated on a trade route more or less halfway between Sub-Saharan Africa and the more Mediterranean-oriented people of the north. It was also within trekking distance west to Kenya, to Nairobi and Mombassa, not a problem for the Nomadic people who walked the bush endlessly with their tents and children and camels and goats. The Nomads have limitless endurance, except, of course, in times of genocidal strife, as these times surely were.

Huddur had been virtually destroyed during the civil war. It had a few remaining buildings with roofs, white-washed, pock-marked affairs, windowless and listing slightly. The large open room where the clan leaders were waiting for us was dark and cool, filled with heavily armed men all talking at once, brushing their brilliant white teeth with sticks and chewing *cat.* The minute we stepped inside, the room went dead quiet, and we took our seats, without any fuss or introduction, near the two pretty French nurses from Médecins Sans Frontières (MSF). We were near the front, and everybody, it seemed, gazed at me, as though I had the answer. Of course, I had nothing of the sort.

"They know you're a Yank, Yank." Sean Lee winked, elbowing me.

On that note and without any warning, as if on cue, automatic gunfire erupted, coming from somewhere outside, and the room was strafed repeatedly, high up on the walls, shredding the roof beams. I thought immediately that the shooting was meant to scare, not to kill. The firing was so prolonged, though, that the room filled up with a rank, chemical gun smoke, a blue cloud that hung above us as we were yanked from under our benches and led out a tiny side door at gunpoint, crawling and crab-walking back into the bright, blinding light of mid-morning. We were thrown roughly up against a crumbling side wall running along a narrow, feces-littered yard, and then ordered, in Arabic, to face the wall and to put our hands above our heads.

This turned out to be my official welcome to Somalia. It was the first of four equally official kidnappings, but it was also how I met my bodyguard. He came around the corner with five other young gunmen, all of them firing at once. The young man who'd taken us hostage immediately threw down his weapon, threw his hands up in the air, and started screaming and pleading at the top of his lungs as Sean Lee and I and the French nurses all hit the ground at once amid the barking dogs and ricocheting bullets and confused shouting coming from inside the building we'd just evacuated. The man who'd taken us captive then bolted, leaving his weapon and running down the alley at a fair clip. My bodyguard then raised his weapon, took very careful aim, and picked him off just as he tried to make a sharp right turn and dart around a corner. Shot in the foot, he hit the dirt hard, face first, then came up fast with a surprised smile on his face, dragged himself out of the line of fire, and disappeared. Sean Lee, who apparently knew a lot more about what was going on than anybody else, was also smiling. He was grinning from ear to ear, as a matter of fact. He gallantly pulled the French nurses to their feet, dusted them off, escorted them past the milling, chattering clan leaders, and helped them up into the Jeep.

As soon as my bodyguard—this crack shot, *this grinning little boy* with his very own automatic weapon, his very own Kalashnikov that was almost as big as he was, whose business end was still smoking—gave Sean Lee a knowing nod, he and his young mates piled onto the back and we roared off down what was left of Huddur's main drag. Bleached out by the noonday heat, it looked to me a lot like one of those old Hollywood movie set ghost towns, the ones you find by following the billboards out in the Nevada desert. Sean Lee was now driving hell's bells directly into the path of a sheer, oncoming wall of tin-cup-brandishing humanity, a half-clothed sea of mud-colored skeletons. With my bodyguard barking orders at them at gunpoint, ordering them to move out of our way and, on more than one occasion, personally pole-axing the disobedient with the scarred wooden butt of his weapon, they parted just barely enough for the Jeep to roll slowly through. They touched us gently, and laughed, and all talked at once, and had perfect teeth. All of them—the men *and* the women—looked just like Iman and Waris Durie, the

internationally famous Somali models, except that these people were, to a one, lethally underweight and wrapped in rags. The little children, all distended bellies and swollen heads, giggled and gently brushed my face and the bushy bleached hair on my arms, playful, their eyes alive with curiosity, their hands outstretched, calling out funny stuff like "Michael Jackson, Michael Jackson." I looked up, and my bodyguard actually winked at me, then held up his hand, palm outstretched, and waited.

"High five, high five, ya dumb Yank," Sean Lee barked.

He then slapped my bodyguard's outstretched palm. I followed suit, too, the first high five of my career. Sean Lee gunned the Jeep. We pushed on through the mob without running anybody over, dropped the French nurses off at their compound, a makeshift pediatric clinic on the edge of Huddur, where hundreds of emaciated children ran around and around in the dust, kicking soccer balls, and then we drove onto Concern headquarters, a modest little two-room Italianate villa, amply supplied with crates of imported spaghetti, bottled water, and cash, but without a single stick of furniture except for a battered dining table and some cots, a bright blue waterproof tarp for a roof, and a courtyard surrounded by a cementblock wall topped by shards of broken glass. A Concern banner and the Irish flag were lashed to a pole.

The gate was manned by Nassar, an ink-black, cigarettesmoking guard sporting a turban and criss-crossed bandolier. He was a dead ringer for Humphrey Bogart. He would soon become my driver.

While Sean Lee gathered up his belongings and stuffed them into some rucksacks, and with my bodyguard trailing close behind us both and watching me closely, he showed me how to use the shortwave radio, my lifeline to Mogadishu. As

Patrick Dillon in Somalia.(Courtesy Patrick Dillon)

he finished packing, he laid out the modest little list of my responsibilities, the foremost of which was to get the airstrip patched up as quickly as I could. Almost every one of Somalia's roads had been heavily damaged by the fighting and was virtually impassable. The only way in or out of Huddur, in terms of supply lines, was by air, and until the airstrip was properly repaired, graded, and secured, none of the bigger contracting cargo planes–the flying C.I.A. truck drivers from Air America, or even military aircraft–would even consider landing on it. I was also supposed to finish setting up the feeding centers and outfit them for cooking rice, beans, and maize, two meals per day for anywhere between thirty thousand and fifty thousand people. There were also extremely serious sanitation problems. The unburied dead were piling up like cordwood along with tons of raw sewage, and if that wasn't sorted out soon we'd have enough pestilence on our hands to wipe everybody out, food or no food. Lastly, there was a single potable well, whose water had already been, according to Sean's rudimentary tests, seriously compromised by all kinds of bacteria, since everybody, despite Sean's repeated attempts to discourage them, used it for everything. As a result, diarrhea and its even more evil stepchild, dysentery, were already rife. A new well had to be drilled. There was still a fair amount of water underground, but the water table had dropped precipitously due to the drought.

"Is that all? Shii," I joked. "Nope, Yank, it's not. There's the technicals, the cowboys you've been seein' every night on the telly."

He was referring to the free-lancing ex-guerrillas who'd made the nightly news by rolling around Somalia in RayBans and Toyota pickups mounted with anti-aircraft guns, raiding whatever foodstuffs or supplies were being imported from the so-called First World, and then reselling the stuff at top dollar in Mogadishu and Baidoa, Somalia's second biggest city.

They were what the thirty thousand heavily armed United States Marines coming ashore at Mogadishu were ostensibly all about.

"They've showed up here, too. They keep raiding my warehouse, and nobody can stop them, not the UN, not even their own people. Maybe your wee fellas'll do the trick, 'From the Halls of Montezuma.' The cowboys, they hit our place again two days ago, kidnapped the guard, and took almost all the cooking oil we had left in there. They're tough wee bastards and like yer man here."

He nodded at Muhammad Ali.

"They know that as long as they can out-gun everybody, them and theirs, they'll eat. The rest, the Nomads in the camps you saw on the way in, they're workin' on raw maize right now. It rips 'em apart, inside like, it just races right through 'em, and they keep foockin' eatin' it even though it's killin' 'em. That and the bloody measles. UNICEF pulled out last week. Said it was too dicey for 'em. Took all their measles vaccine away with 'em, too, they did. Try and rig the feeding centers up with some boilers, the bigger the better, like they do back home for the spuds. Boilin' the water'll kill off some o' the bacteria *and* cook the rice and beans. *If* you can find fuel. The rest is up to you, Yank, you and the baby Jesus. Americans, they're world famous for figurin' things out, so go right ahead, have a whack. And if you use that brain o' yours for somethin' besides a hatbox, you'll let the Somalis them-selves carry the lion's share of the load. They may look like they're on the balls of their arses, and they are, but they're also strong and smart, the women too, them even more so than the men. Any one o' them can drop the engine block outta one o' them-there Russian-made trucks, straighten out the crank shaft, and throw it right back up inside—with their foockin' *fingertips*. Oh, yeah. One last tip—don't drink the water. Now, take me out to that plane, if you please, before that auld UN wanker decides he's waited long enough in this godforsaken place and flies back to Nairobi without me."

On the way out to the airport, we stopped at a small enclave of interconnected, mud-covered huts that resembled oversized beehives, the home of Hassan Waddi Hassan, the tireless, Eddie Murphy-quoting, *cat*-chewing Concern translator. Hassan's English was more or less fluent. He also spoke Italian, Spanish, and German, the result of wearing out stacks of bootlegged American and European movie videos, the odd correspondence course, and a very brief stay as a student *boulevardier* in Italy, Somalia's last colonial conquistador. Hassan jumped into the back and high-fived my bodyguard. We drove past the local burial grounds, acres and acres of very fresh and equally shallow graves, each one marked by a few stones or the odd religious figurine. A small crew of gravediggers were hard at work even though the sun was almost directly above us now and pushing the thermometer toward 120 degrees. The dead were laid out in rows, separated by age, gender, and clan, and family members huddled around the fresh graves, praying quietly or weeping.

"You'll have to get a handle on that one quick, Yank, yesterday like. Call up Mog and put in an emergency request for more picks, shovels, and wheelbarrows, and put some new teams on the case, or just start burnin' 'em. Nobody's gonna like that. Not one bit. Hassan?"

"Not burning. Very bad religion. More shroud cloth," he said.

"More shroud cloth it is," Sean said.

He cast a sideways glance at me as he concurred.

"They should make Hassan president."

Hassan nodded approvingly.

"Or ambassador to Ireland, at the very least."

We drove on. Soon we heard the high-pitched whine of airplane engines revving up, and then the airstrip appeared

Milk being distributed to refugee children in Somalia. (UN Photo 146 504/Peter Magubane)

in the distance, undulating in the pounding heat. The plane was there, about to take off. Sean was leaving, and I was staying. I turned, and my bodyguard winked at me, put his hand on my shoulder to steady himself when we bottomed out suddenly on some mortar craters that pock-marked the airstrip, and then whispered something to Hassan.

"He wants to know if you're a millionaire, like everybody else in America," Hassan said. "Tell him I have a tee shirt back home that says, *'Fight Hunger, Eat the Rich.'*"

We rolled to a stop not far from the plane. The pilot

waved. Hassan grabbed Sean's bags, slung them on his shoulders, and walked out of earshot.

"They told me all about you, Yank," Sean said to me, by way of departing words. "That you were a medic in Vietnam, and were in Cuba and Central America and the Peace Corps, and Belfast, as well, as a matter of fact. I won't ask you why you went to any o' them crazy places, not even the Six Counties. I'm sure you had your reasons. But of all the crazy places you've been, there's none as crazy as this one. Or as sad. I'll wish you all the best of luck. Keep your head down and do what those fellas say."

He nodded toward Hassan, and then stuck a thumb in the direction of the Jeep, where Humphrey Bogart silently smoked a Marlboro and my bodyguard wiped down his weapon with a rag.

"You'll do just fine. Ta, Yank."

With that, and a laugh and a handshake, Sean Lee flew away, leaving us all with our heads bent low inside a blinding cloud of stinging red dirt, jet wash, and exhaust fumes. The plane was swallowed up quickly inside a sky bleached white by a sun that was already popping red spots in front of my eyes and hot little blisters on my lips.

You've really gone and done it this time, haven't you? How are you going to get out of this one alive, huh, mister high-and-mighty? Just who do you think you are, huh, Batman? You couldn't save anybody in the 'Nam. Not one single goddamn bleeder. Now, you're going to save Somalia?

HOW TO DESCRIBE the next six months? *Pornographic* is the only English word that comes close. Soft-core, not the hard stuff, at least not until the end. That was a snuff film. My bodyguard, Muhammad Ali, *just like the Champ,* lived underneath the Jeep. I never saw him eat, I never saw him sleep, I never saw him shit, and I never saw him cry, except for once,

when he confessed, through Hassan, that he'd somehow
managed to lose the Swiss Army knife I'd given him as a
Christmas present. I think he expected me to punish him,
perhaps even relieve him of duty, or beat him. Instead, I
hugged him and, when I did this, he burst out in big, rolling,
little boy sobs. Then he caught himself up and ran away and
didn't come back until Hassan and Humphrey Bogart went
and coaxed him out of his hiding place inside the abandoned
airstrip building where we stored the hundreds and hundreds
of rusted, unexploded mines we found on a regular basis, all
over Huddur.

My bodyguard's people proved to be some of the most
resourceful, heroic, and tragic human beings I will ever
know. Somehow, the measles plague ran its course, dying out
eventually as all plagues do. Somehow, the dead babies got
buried, and other babies were born. Somehow, my bodyguard's people managed to rebuild the airstrip–by hand–and
then we got regular food flights into Huddur, sometimes as
many as five per day. Somehow–with the help of a chain-
smoking Algerian journalist, Bushan Achmed ul-Haq, hired
on as an official observer by the World Food Program–we
negotiated a deal with the technicals, paying them in rice and
beans to ride shotgun on our convoys as we started pushing
food and displaced people back out into the bush, a stop-gap
measure taken to stem the relentless tide of in-migration that
was overwhelming our meager resources. Somehow, we
organized a small army of wheelbarrow-and-shovel-wielding
women into sanitation teams, paying them promptly, and
with dignified solemnity, every Friday afternoon, with stacks
of elegantly engraved and virtually worthless Somali money.
Somehow, we got the herders to stop slaughtering the last of
their precious camels, these obscene acts of carnage they
unveiled for all to see right smack in the middle of the roads.
This was near the end, after Mogadishu began to go up in

Women and children await food distribution at a UNICEF feeding center in Baidoa, a town northwest of Mogadishu. (UNICEF/5534/Wendy Stone)

flames, after the French Foreign Legion showed up in Huddur without warning and with ridiculous—and extremely dangerous—notions about disarming some of the most heavily armed human beings, pound for pound, on the planet.

The camel-killing was a shocking, anguished, suicidal decision on the part of the Nomads. It was driven by madness, by hunger, and by some sort of entrepreneurial fever dream. They macheted their most priceless assets to pieces and then put them up for sale at the market, fly-covered heads and hooves and all, right next to the stolen European Union bags of rice and beans, leaving pools of bright red camel blood and entrails in their wake, great, fetid, coagulating lakes cheesing over in the sun and tromped through by little shoeless children.

Somehow, we managed to bury the dead and to keep the living alive, at least for a while.

A lot of the very terrifying things that were done to me during those six months were, it turned out, a very elaborate form of Japanese Noh theater, tailored very specifically to bring me around to the Somali way of thinking, to teach me some extremely important lessons about bush survival, clan logic and culture, rather than to harm or even kill me, however close they did come, on numerous occasions, to doing both. And even though my bodyguard was a part of that great, wounded, unknowable, African *Other*–and by far the youngest member of my crew–the most miraculous aspect of our bond was that by virtue of some primal, experiential instinct, Muhammad Ali, *just like the Champ,* quickly became the organizing principle around which my life was prolonged, repeatedly, over some of the strangest–and most transformational–weeks and months of my life. In this way, it became clear to me–and even more so now, a decade on– that my bodyguard knew instinctively something his elders either didn't, or out of arrogance or madness or superstition, simply refused to believe: Without me actually *standing* out there in the middle of that airstrip every single morning, at first light, waving my walkie-talkie at that prayed-for first food flight of the day making its initial ground-hugging, ear-shattering security fly-by, there would be no food. However many echoes of colonial criminality this invokes–and there are many, believe me–my bodyguard knew that by keeping me alive he was keeping not only himself alive, but his people, his clan, and Somalia itself. Those were just *the rules,* an unspoken, Faustian bargain my bodyguard and I had, a symbiotic pact we kept, like blood brothers, one that drove me on and drove Muhammad Ali to protect me at all costs—shoot first and ask questions later—through any number of dead-of-night firefights and three other full-blown, adrenaline-soaked, gun-at-your-head kidnappings.

With my bodyguard watching my back, I began to feel as though I was charmed. I began wading like some comic book character into gun-wielding mobs threatening to tear each other apart over bags of beans or rumors or things I wasn't doing the right way or their way or *the clan* way, facing down any number of hardened, hollow-cheeked food rustlers, young Rambos howling at me in Arabic with the business ends of their hair-trigger Armalites inches from my sun-blistered face, and screaming right back at them until we were all laughing and tear-stained and holding hands and hoarse. So when my bodyguard got sick and died, so quickly, so did Somalia, and so did I.

He rolled out from underneath the Jeep one morning with his right eye swollen completely shut and half his face an angry, reddened hive. With what little bottled water I had on hand I washed his eye out, bandaged it up as best as I could with a field kit, and then we high-tailed it out to the MSF clinic, where the Frenchies clucked and whispered in French and nodded gravely as only the French can do. They said they'd seen a lot of it already going around the camps. They gave my bodyguard the full treatment, and he loved it. They hugged him and kissed him and made him laugh while they washed his eye out again, with saline solution this time, then swabbed the rash down with betadine solution, before applying a fresh *French* bandage. My bodyguard was grinning from ear to ear and sucking on a sweet when the nurses told me they'd run dangerously low on antibiotics and couldn't spare even a single dose of ampicillin. They said they hoped to be resupplied by their people in Mog within the week, that it was probably nothing to worry too much about, a virus and a low-level infection, and that it would, like a lot of other things weird and wonderful out here in bush country, simply run its course.

But my bodyguard, Muhammad Ali, *just like the Champ,* he died anyway, two days later, from a high fever and an infection of unknown origin that probably entered his beautiful little brain through his bloodstream, and from rubbing his eye all the time just like I told him not to, just like all kids do, and from not having a dose of rudimentary medicine that costs about as much as a Tootsie Roll.

He seemed to shake it off at first, like a movie tough guy, and by the end of that day the swelling even appeared to go down a bit. But then, on the following very chilly morning, after Hassan and I listened anxiously, before dawn, to the first unconfirmed reports on the shortwave about UN peace-keeper killings and firefights raging in and around Mogadishu, and wondered aloud how this would affect our food flights, we drifted outside at first light and my body-guard, he didn't roll out from underneath the Jeep sleepily, as usual, throwing off the woolen Irish Army blanket with the harp insignia, stretching his arms wide, moaning dreamily, then taking a shy sip of my tea and thanking me politely for it. Even though I became worried about him immediately, I was also, to tell you the truth, a little relieved, too, thinking that my bodyguard had decided to lay low, for once, to take the day, as they say. I knew that his father had been killed in the war, and that his mother had taken flight to Mogadishu with his six brothers, but that he still had an extended family living along with other members of his clan, the Habr Gidr, out by the airstrip feeding center. I made a mental note to check on him before racing through another crisis-crazed day. I never got to do this because I was either at our warehouse inventorying our dwindling foodstuffs or else on the blower, off and on, for the next twenty-four hours, pleading with anybody I could in officialdom not to stop our food from coming in, despite the hostilities suddenly engulfing other parts of Somalia. I dropped into my cot, in a semi-coma and still fully clothed, at around 3 a.m. Hassan woke me well after the sun came up to tell me that all food flights had, in fact, been canceled until further notice on orders from Admiral Howe, the Clinton administration's born-again Christian military commander, who'd once said, on his first day on the job, at a Mogadishu press conference, "Inside a every one a these here Somali people is an American just waitin' ta git out, an' we're here ta help 'em do just that."

Hassan and I immediately started running numbers and quickly concluded that with no flights, within a week we'd probably have between fifteen thousand and twenty-five thousand corpses on our hands, that it could easily wind up being worse than Baidoa, four hours to the southwest, the dead city that had become the world's magazine cover poster child for the Somali diaspora.

With no planes to meet, we drank tea and sized up the day. Then a young runner came barreling into the compound, forced his way past Humphrey Bogart, and ran straight into the house. He was crying and babbling. Hassan finally had to shake him hard and threaten to hit him to get him to calm him down. He was Muhammad Ali's cousin. We were to come quick because my bodyguard, he was very sick. We jumped into the Jeep and my bodyguard's cousin led the way, out past the outdoor movie theater and the graveyard and the airstrip and beyond it, to a ramshackle compound made of dozens of small beehive huts and sheet-plastic tents, all strung together precariously and surrounded by a high, intricately woven fence made of reedy saplings sewn into a mesh with dried vines. All the women—and even some of the men, the older ones—were weeping. Hassan grabbed my

Children waiting for food outside a UNICEF/Swede Relief feeding center in Mogadishu. (UN Photo 159382/M. Grant)

elbow and glanced at me sideways, shaking his head. He knew. I guess I knew, too, but I was fighting it in the way all madmen fight the truth.

A grizzled elder approached me, cocked his head, placed both his gnarled hands over mine, then shrugged and said something softly in Arabic. Hassan introduced him. He was my bodyguard's grandfather, and he was thanking me for taking such good care of his grandson. I wanted to tell him how wrong he was, but I said nothing. He led us past the women, one of whom began to sing. She was reading from the Qur'an, she was *singing* the Qur'an, and when she finished the verse, the others around her sang it back to her. I realized that this was the sound, the song of death, that had been lulling me to sleep every night for months.

I did not want to go inside the hut. My bodyguard—Muhammad Ali, *just like the Champ*—he was in there, and he was dead.

His grandfather beckoned. We went inside.

That afternoon we buried my bodyguard in the yard, with him and his Kalashnikov and his prayer beads and his Nikes sewn inside two used rice bags emptied out and rinsed clean. One of the bags had "Product of Ohio" stamped on its side in red and blue, along with an American flag. I didn't know they grew rice in Ohio, did you, dear reader? Once my bodyguard was laid out and then down inside the fresh-cut hole, and covered with a layer of small stones, I was given the honor, by the head of his clan, an old man with a snubbed-nose .38 police special on his hip, of tossing in the first handful of dirt. I did so, then stood back, crossed my arms, and broiled in the sun while the hole was shoveled full. A lot of people were weeping—even Hassan, even though he and my bodyguard bickered constantly like an old married couple, like my mother and father.

And that's pretty much the end of the story. I never got to drill that second well, something I feel bad about to this very day, because one day about two weeks later, with vicious food fights breaking out all day long and thousands and thousands of Nomads dropping down dead in the dirt, some Concern higher-ups showed up, unannounced, arriving on the MSF resupply flight. They took one long look at me and immediately declared me a human disaster area. I guess they were right. I was forty pounds underweight, shitting water, and covered with parasitic skin lesions from one end of me to the other. They medivaced me out, unceremoniously, and I spent the next month or so in a Nairobi hospital being stuffed back together like Dorothy's friend the Scarecrow after the flying monkeys got through with him. While I was recuperating, I thought a lot about my bodyguard, Muhammad Ali, *just like the Champ*. Dear reader, *he was ten*.

7 *My Testimony*
Bosnia

Maria Blacque-Belair

"I became friendly with people on the street—an old woman, a young boy. And without these attachments I don't know how I would have gotten through these four years. The war was personal for me."

1992-1996. These are the years I spent in Bosnia as an emergency relief worker. Four years of war. I thought I was going to write about why there was a war in Bosnia, why people in the same family, neighbors, killed each other. But I still don't understand. So I might as well drop the pretense of even trying to understand.

Still, I feel an obligation to record what happened for the sake of what the French call *témoignage*–testimony, speaking out. I know that as the years go by, I will forget. And I am also worried that my testimony, and that of others, will not help prevent another war like this. Did the testimony of the survivors of World War II prevent Bosnia?

Before I became a relief worker, I was a journalist. What frustrated me was that I was only an observer. I was covering the UN, and I would listen to people talking about their work in the field, and there I was only asking questions. I knew I had to make a change. It took me a while to understand this.

When I was a child in Morocco, though they were French, my parents were very involved with the independence movement, and in our house there was always a lot of political discussion. My parents are very interesting people.

Maria Blacque-Belair at the airport in Sarajevo, 1993. (Courtesy Maria Blacque-Belair)

Before they married, my mother was a nun and my father was training for the priesthood and worked with the poor in Beirut. They had known each other before, and then at some point they reunited and decided to renounce their vows and get married. Later, we moved to New York, and my father worked as an economist for the UN, specializing in African development. So a philosophy of engagement and interest in the world, serving the world, came naturally to me.

When I am in the field, I do not have time or inclination to write letters. My friends complain bitterly about this. So these words are the beginning of the letter I never wrote to them during those four years in Bosnia:

In February 1992, I had just returned from Iraq, where I had been sent by the French relief organization EquiLibre to start school feeding programs. Before that I was in Romania providing relief in the now notorious orphanages that were more like prisons. This had been a hard assignment for me, to watch children being abused, and today I wonder if we accomplished much there. I didn't leave with a happy heart. From Romania I went to Iraq, which was demanding but not as heart-stopping as the work in Romania. And when I returned to France after Romania, I was asked if I would like to go to Sarajevo. I had to look at a map to figure out where it was. A month later I was there.

The initial assignment was for three weeks. I went with a colleague, Michelle Keane. We landed in Belgrade, where we took two rooms at a hotel in the city center, close to the offices of the UN High Commissioner for Refugees (UNHCR). Our mission was to facilitate flour transportation for refugees in Bosnia who had fled the conflict between Serbia and Croatia. We met with officials of UNHCR to fig- ure out the best ways to organize these convoys. They greet- ed us warmly, though they were a bit surprised by the timing of our visit. "Don't you know there will be a war here?" they asked us. We thought they were pulling our leg.

From Belgrade we took a small plane to Sarajevo. Everything seemed so peaceful then. Every night we were invited out, usually to the old town—the Muslim area—which looked like a piece of Turkey displaced in the middle of Europe. It was magical, full of dim lights all over the mosques dotting the hills surrounding the town. Young people and old were strolling on the streets, greeting each other, sitting in cafés and sipping the famous Sarajevan coffee. Shops were filled with goods—dry fruits, candies, pistachios. There were so many stunning women, all fashionably dressed. How could there be a war here, I asked myself. But from one day to the next, it happened. The UN recognized Bosnia Herzegovina's independence, and before even the official declaration, the Serbs attacked.

It was a Saturday, April 4, 1992. I was awakened by shots and explosions. I went downstairs and the concierge told me, "Don't worry, this is the end of Ramadan. Everyone shoots in the air. It's our tradition." But she was wrong.

Within minutes the Medécins San Frontières (MSF) team, who had been living in the hills, came storming into our hotel, frightened, because the hills were already not safe. During that weekend I helped them retrieve their belongings from their house and, on Sunday, we were all in the MSF office when we started to hear sirens and taxis driving full speed. They were transporting wounded people. There was shooting everywhere, barricades were going up, snipers killing peace demonstrators in front of the Holiday Inn Hotel. Suddenly we were in the middle of a war.

I spent most of my time with the MSF workers because they had cars and radios. Every day all the relief workers in town met at a Chinese restaurant and discussed logistics. Within days, journalists' cars were being stolen by the Serbs, militias were roaming everywhere, there was no hot water, and food was becoming scarce.

There was so much activity in the following weeks. US planes arrived with medical supplies and food rations, but everyone was afraid to unload, fearing snipers. I was not afraid for some reason and, together with a colleague, I unloaded the planes for a whole afternoon and came back to the hotel exhausted. Then Bernard Kouchner, founder of MSF, arrived to evacuate the children of Sarajevo. Every day we ferried children to the airport who were being sent to relatives either in Croatia or Serbia. It was sad to see these separation scenes, especially to see grandmothers saying good-bye to their grandchildren. It was as if they knew better than the others that it would be a long separation.

How often did I leave the hotel in those weeks under gun-fire? How often did we have to sleep in the entrance hall because of the heavy shelling? I cannot remember now.

Life is bizarre during a war. One night we were invited to General Morillon's for dinner. He was the commander of the UN Protection Force (UNPROFOR). The city was being heavily shelled; nonetheless, we had a perfect dinner served in the general's residence by waiters in white gloves. Bernard Kouchner played the piano and sang; all of us were quiet and a bit drunk. We felt as if we were on a sinking ship. Around us, the city was going up in flames.

We continued our work, trying to evacuate as many children as possible from small, traditionally Muslim villages that were so quickly surrounded by Serb forces. The airport was no longer reachable, and it was becoming increasingly difficult to move around. No supplies could be delivered, so there was nothing more we could do. Finally, we were forced, reluctantly, to evacuate the city. All the organizations decided it was much too dangerous to stay there. I was one of the last relief workers to leave, and though I knew it was necessary, I look upon this decision with remorse. Sarajevo was left alone, to fend for itself.

I could not wait to return. I set up a logistical base in Zagreb and then Split, and counted the days. But it wasn't until April 1993 that I saw Sarajevo again. I returned to the city as project director for Action Internationale Contre la Faim (AICF), and my job was now a big one—to launch a relief program for the victims of what had become a war-torn country.

Getting an office together after a year of war was quite a challenge. There was nothing in the city: no paper, no supplies, no desks, and no chairs. But my colleague Mabrouk Brahmi was incredibly resourceful and had a wonderful good-natured personality. Born in Lyons of Algerian parents, he was twenty-eight years old when I met him. Still so young. Several days after our arrival, he found everything we needed. Among his vast network of friends, Mabrouk had gotten to know General Morillon's personal cook. Often the cook would come to our office with paté de foie gras and other delicacies. In exchange, we let him use our satellite phone so he could call his girlfriend back in France. These small day-to-day niceties warmed us and gave us the strength to continue our work.

Sixty soldiers from the UN Egyptian battalion were housed on the same floor as our offices. We shared the same bathroom, and I must say it was sometimes a bit tense as they washed their feet in the sink a few times a day before going to their "mosque," a room on another floor. There was very little water available, about an hour in the morning and again for an hour at night. So water was scarce, and we did not like it that the men mostly used it to wash their feet, which meant there was none left to wash our faces. But we didn't complain at all because we felt privileged to have water a few hours a day, which none of the citizens of Sarajevo had.

I did complain once to the commander of the Egyptian battalion when one of his soldiers tried to kiss my colleague Anne, our water engineer. His answer was, "I do not understand what you are doing here. You should be at home having babies." I don't remember my reply.

I became friendly with people on the street—an old woman, a young boy. And without these attachments I don't know how I would have gotten through these four years. The war was personal for me. Some might say I over-identify and that I suffer from bystander guilt. I know this is true. When I am next to people who are suffering, I must do something. I have no choice. I feel so lucky that this is not my family, not

In 1996, people of Gorazde meet the first buses to arrive from Sarajevo: a symbol of resurrection after many months of suffering and isolation. (UNHCR/R. LeMoyne)

my grandmother, not my mother. And this is the motivation for action. I really think that I didn't have post-traumatic stress or even burn-out because of this, because of my relationships and my passion for the work. It was tiring and dangerous, but the feedback of knowing we made a difference even in one person's life was so satisfying.

By the end of September 1993 the war had escalated again, and we could feel the winter descending harshly on Sarajevo. The Bosnian Parliament had rejected the latest peace plan, so the water and electricity were completely cut off once again. I was living with John Fawcett, my future husband, and we had moved into a new apartment hoping we would have more privacy. But this was impossible. The only hotel in town, the Holiday Inn, was full-up with journalists and very expensive. So we had a constant stream of house guests, mostly other relief workers.

Like the citizens, I was getting used to the privations of Sarajevo. How adaptable we are. We slept in a bedroom without heat, and thank God, we had warm sleeping bags. To get wood was a big job, and it was also very expensive. AICF paid for it, which was not the case for the people of Sarajevo. Most of them resorted to burning books, furniture, even clothes, to warm themselves.

I began to feel the contradictions of our work. Sarajevo felt like a prison that winter, and the relief workers were the guards. "Do you feed us so we can die with a fat belly?" people asked us. It was difficult to answer this question because we felt that our governments were using our presence on the ground as an excuse for inaction. But we felt it was our duty to stay and to advocate—to scream—that military and political intervention was necessary. And, despite this dilemma, we had to keep working, escaping bullets at close range to bring food and blankets to old people, for example. We also started to do repairs in the dozens of refugee sites in the city: fixing roofs, water systems, toilets. We tried to make people a little more comfortable in the besieged city.

Christmas arrived and the city was buried under snow. In spite of everything, Sarajevo had not lost its joie de vivre, for which it was famous before the war. People would stay up all night because the 10 p.m. curfew was too early to stop having fun. Sometimes I felt ill at ease with all the partying, even though I liked to dance all night myself, knowing each night could be my last. And there was a sexual frenzy, too. When we asked our local staff members if they needed something from the outside world, a common request was condoms. But as the war dragged on, the frenzy diminished. It was no longer a good way to forget.

I was feeling afraid sometimes and afraid to go out. This was new for me. On February 4, 1994, I decided to force myself to leave the office, to brave my fear. Otherwise, I thought I would never be able to go out on the streets again. So I asked my driver to go to the market with me. I remember telling him, "Please park the car close by, in case something happens."

There was absolutely nothing in the market that day: a few potatoes, coffee at an incredibly high price, smuggled meat. A kilo of veal cost more than a hundred dollars. I always refused to buy such items because I totally despised the black marketers who took advantage of their fellow citizens in this shameful way. I looked at this produce and told my driver, "We might as well go back to the office."

It took about fifteen minutes by car to get back to the office, and when I returned, it was like entering a funeral parlor. The staff members were crying hysterically and frantically calling members of their families. They told me that a massacre had taken place at the market and more than sixty people had been cut into pieces by shrapnel. Fortunately, none of the families of our local staff had been wounded. And I realized how lucky I had been. I must have left the market just minutes before the explosion. And I had traveled there to brave my fear.

The next day, I went to the UNPROFOR press briefing. The UN "denounced" the massacre but said it could not point the finger at who did it for lack of evidence. The Serbs said that the Bosnians did it to themselves. So, in a shell-shocked city, the wildest rumors were circulating. And that was a terrible stress in itself.

Amidst rows of destroyed buildings, a street sign advising caution for passing school children stands riddled with bullets near the dividing line between eastern and western sides of the war-torn Bosnian city of Mostar. (UNICEF/94-0881/Roger LeMoyne)

A few days later we learned that the international community had given the Serbs an ultimatum, insisting that they pull back their guns. At last something was happening that sounded more solid than usual. I must say that all of us felt very relieved. Finally, under the leadership of the Americans and Richard Holbrooke, a political solution was imposed over a humanitarian approach. And then the Dayton Agreement was signed. Suddenly, we had visitors roaming around in the formerly besieged city hungering for a glimpse of what war was like. The Sarajevans themselves were not jumping with joy because they had been so disappointed so many times and were so exhausted. They were still walking miles to fetch water.

Our project director arrived from Zagreb to boost our morale, as she said proudly. She had gone on vacation three times during the war, so she was in great spirits. I did not feel this was enough support for what we had done.

John and I wanted to go to New York for a while and immerse ourselves in "normal life." Our goal was to learn about the Internet because we had felt so cut off for so long. I felt bad for the friends I was leaving behind in Bosnia because I knew they also wanted to be part of the electronic revolution where there are no borders, flags, or nationalities.

That first winter back in New York was exceptionally cold, and there was the biggest snow storm in a decade. The city's traffic was stopped, and Mayor Giuliani got on TV and advised New Yorkers to stock up on food and water. John and I had to smile hearing this. We had heat in our apartment. We had hot water. There were no bombs. What was everyone complaining about? And it felt strange to hear news reports about the American soldiers landing in Bosnia, the cold winter there, their flimsy tents. No one felt sorry for us when we had to work in the ongoing war, day after day.

It has taken me a long time to get over these feelings of anger at the outside world. My studies at New York University have helped a lot. If I am going to do clinical work with survivors, I must master these complicated feelings. And they are very complicated. For two years after the war, I sheltered myself, hardly going to parties or talking to people other than relief workers. When I did go out, I had to force myself not to talk about Bosnia and to be interested in other people.

It is hard to come to any conclusion about my four years in Bosnia. Perhaps it will take a long time to digest what happened to that beautiful country, and what happened to me when I was there. Many strong feelings and images remain. But mostly I remember the people, other relief workers, and two Bosnian women in particular who became my friends, Souada Kapic and Vesna Cengic. I would like to pay homage to them here:

To Vesna Cengic, a doctor who worked throughout the war in the hospital in Sarajevo. She speaks perfect French and received several offers from French generals to be a personal translator. She refused. For Vesna, it was very clear. She was a doctor, and her duty was to treat the wounded and dying.

To Souada Kapic, a television producer. When the war broke out she was in Belgrade. Instead of remaining in this safe haven, she returned to Sarajevo and became one of the most important figures in the cultural resistance. She began a survival museum, cultural newsletters, and a survival guide.

It took four years for the international community to intervene in this terrible war. In Kosovo it took three months. So there is hope.

8 *The Tremor Within*
Liberia

Paul E. Arès

"What am I doing here? How did we get caught up in this mess? I hope nobody gets hurt. How painful it would be for our families if we got killed. What would it be like to get shot? How would it feel?"

When the first signs came, I thought I had simply picked up a bug of some kind. It was odd, like a vibration or tremor deep inside my body. I thought that antibiotics would take care of it. When the symptoms persisted and got stronger, I went to the next stage of the analysis. Was this caused by a tumor, an ulcer, or some kind of tropical parasite? Over the next year and a half I went through every conceivable test, and they all came out negative. I was convinced that I, of all people, did not have a psychological problem. The doctor at the UN told me otherwise; I was suffering from post-traumatic stress disorder.

It's not necessarily one single incident, or event, that will take your body to the precipice, but rather an accumulation of suppressed feelings, pain, denials, and shock. I'd been going into the field for many years and thought, assumed, I could cope with anything. As a manager I never sent my workers anywhere I did not go myself and considered safe. I did not consider how I was endangered, physically and emotionally, when I was on these missions. Until Liberia.

SOMETIMES THERE IS a ceasefire; at other times there is simply an understanding with the government or a rebel group

A girl with her grandmother in a refugee camp in Borkeza, Liberia. (UN/DPI Photo by John Isaac)

that the World Food Program (WFP) will be allowed into a designated area with food. This involves intense negotiations with the warring parties, tentative agreements, and the hope that the area is safe enough to distribute much-needed food to the civilian population. Like others who are involved in the preliminary negotiations before going into a war-torn area, there is concern as we set out to meet rebel leaders and warlords to determine the level of risk. Is it tolerable? Is it manageable? Will the ceasefire hold? These are the questions we ask ourselves as we negotiate passage of food convoys into conflict zones. On rare occasions we will accept an escort either from the government or from the rebel group that is controlling the territory.

Food aid becomes a very attractive commodity in conflict areas because everybody is hungry. Sometimes fighters will insist, at gunpoint, that part of the food be given up at check-points in order for them to allow a convoy to continue on its humanitarian mission. It is exceptional, but it does happen. Most often, what is given up is not significant enough to make us turn back. The main objective is to save the lives of those innocent people who are dying of hunger and hunger-related diseases.

Though I worried about my safety and that of my colleagues when working in these areas, the danger never stopped me. I am driven by a desire to help, and my colleagues are driven by the same desire. However, I often said to myself, there is no room for error; the safety of my team is in my hands.

January 1996

We were on a UN Interagency Assessment Mission to the northern part of Liberia to assess the food security situation of the people who lived in Upper Lofa. We had also heard that some Liberian refugees were returning from Guinea to a few of the villages along the border. Before heading to the area, we obtained clearance from the UN field security officer to travel, but only on the condition that one of the faction commanders who "controlled" that area would accompany us. As part of the standard procedure when UN staff travel in insecure areas, we would also be accompanied by an unarmed peacekeeping soldier. He was a Sikh from the Indian Peacekeeping Contingent, which was part of UNOMIL (United Nations Observer Mission in Liberia).

It was early in the morning when five of us climbed aboard a UNOMIL helicopter along with the Sikh peacekeeper and a fighter who went by the name of General Combat. As one member of the mission remarked, he was our "living passport" into the area. Just before boarding, we all signed a document releasing the UN of all responsibility. This is an indemnity document; if something goes wrong, families will be compensated, but the UN is not liable in the event of a lawsuit.

I often think of this helicopter ride. It was like being on a roller coaster. We flew just above the trees, up and down the hills, as we made our way through fighting zones. It was exhilarating! My breath stopped as my heart jolted forward. The scenery was beautiful: virgin jungle below, tall trees, flocks of birds lifting and flowing away as we passed over, the occasional river, and someone fishing from a dugout canoe. And then, the occasional burned-out village—a stern reminder of why we were on this mission.

We landed close to the village of Vajun and walked in to meet with the chief and some of the elders. I was impressed as a throng of kids and teenagers crowded around General Combat, all looking at him in awe. Some were touching him, others trying to talk to him, all just wanting to be beside him. I asked one of the kids why he was so special to them. He was from this village and was revered as one of the strongest fighters because he had killed many people to achieve the

Paul Arès in Liberia. (Courtesy Paul Arès)

rank of general in ULIMO-K, the fighting faction led by
Alhaji Kromah. While we sat and talked to the villagers, I
noticed that he was very quiet and appeared to be sad. Never
did he smile, he just listened in silence. When we left, he
smiled a bit as the villagers accompanied their "hero" back to
the helicopter. We left in a cloud of dust, with kids crouching
down, covering their eyes, or being swept away as the wind
from the turning blades pushed us upward.

Shortly after, we landed in the next village, Voinjama,
and found ourselves completely alone in the middle of what
had once been a soccer field. A little perplexed, since we had

been told that we would be expected, we walked toward the center of the town. There was nobody around. Most of the buildings were either destroyed or abandoned. Finally, someone appeared. He claimed that he was on the town council. We sat with him in the town hall and began asking him questions about refugees and the availability of food and shelter for them. He said there were no refugees, and only bush food was available. Within minutes, a group of armed gunmen, most of them young teenagers, arrived and told us to follow them. We looked at the man from the town council and he shrugged his shoulders, saying that they had the guns and that we had no choice but to follow them.

They escorted us to what had been the local school, which now served as the headquarters for the group of fighters controlling the area. There were many fighters milling about. I smiled at one of them, as I generally do to indicate that I mean them no harm, but he didn't smile. His hair was cut flat on top and rising straight up from the sides. He wore a red beret to one side, a long tee-shirt falling below his hips, and pants cut off below the knees. As with most of the others, flip-flops were his footwear. He carried his large weapon with ease as he motioned me up the stairs.

Once inside, we were herded into one of the classrooms, along with General Combat, and told to wait there. After a while, the "General" was taken away. We all thought that he would straighten this out and that we could go on with our assessment in the village. We waited. As time passed we got more and more worried. We looked at one another, thinking we'd better get ourselves back to the helicopter and out of here. Then, one of the gunmen returned. The gunmen spoke among themselves in a dialect that none of us could understand. Then one of them spoke to us in English, informing us that we were now in their custody and that they could not guarantee our safety.

We protested, explaining that ULIMO-K had given us clearance and that General Combat had come along to ensure that we would be protected and would have full collaboration. The gunmen told us that they had no knowledge that we were coming and that they did not recognize General Combat, who had no authority in this area. Again we protested, but it didn't seem to matter. We explained the purpose of our mission and said that if this was not acceptable to them, we would leave immediately. They said no, that we were in their custody now and must give them our passports.

"We don't have our passports with us," I replied, not wanting to admit that we did in fact have them with us. "We are here to help the people of the village, to bring them food. They are hungry," I continued.

"We don't care. You have no business here," replied one of the gunmen. "Give us your passports."

All the while, the UNOMIL peacekeeper sat silently in the corner watching every move. He didn't have a weapon, and it was probably best that he didn't; it would be interpreted by the fighters as a provocation. Having weapons presupposes a readiness to use them. For this and other reasons, weapons are never allowed on UN helicopters carrying out humanitarian missions.

We refused to give them our passports, and this made some of them angry, but we knew that the CRS (Catholic Relief Services) representative on our assessment team was an American and that she could be at risk.

"Who is American?" asked one of the gunmen.

"We are UN. We don't give our nationalities," I replied.

We refused to give our identities. The gunmen started to argue heatedly among themselves.

Suddenly we heard a voice rise above the others: "You are all a bunch of brats. You don't know what you are doing. You are wrong."

It was one of our group speaking in a very condescending manner. The gunmen turned toward him, startled and menacing.

"Don't pay any attention to him. He's nervous and a bit upset," I said quickly. "Let's talk about solving our problem here."

The younger gunmen were getting quite agitated. We did not need these provocative remarks. It would only make things worse. They had the guns, and they were tense. In such circumstances things can get out of hand for little reason.

I was sitting at the end of the table on a broken chair with no back when one of the gunmen came into the room and waved me away with his AK-47. The chair I was sitting on was for their leader. The leader then walked in and introduced himself as Jungle Boy. Many of them had names like this. We had heard of another one who was known as Butt Naked. He would strip down, cover himself with a special oil, and then go into battle completely naked. He believed the oil had powers to make him invincible, that bullets could not touch him or would simply bounce off him. He survived the war and became a hero to many of the youths who aspired to join militias in Liberia.

Jungle Boy was tall and slim and wore what looked like a .45 Colt in a holster on his hip. He started questioning us again on the purpose of our mission. Then he turned toward General Combat: "You are responsible for these people. You brought them here. We will hold you responsible if they bring trouble."

"I am with them. There is no problem," replied General Combat. "Let them talk to the villagers and then we will all go. They only talk about food."

Jungle Boy smiled and said: "OK. They are free to do their work. They must be gone in two hours."

That was the end of the detainment, a short hostage-taking, and a warning. It had lasted three hours. Unfortunately for the local people, we decided that this area was too insecure for any kind of relief activity.

SOME MONTHS LATER, in the fall of 1996, the civil war in Liberia came to an end with a ceasefire and the implementation of the Abuja Peace Agreement, signed by all parties in August 1995. A transitional authority was put in place to prepare the country for an election to be held in July 1997.

The WFP had continuously provided food aid to needy Liberians throughout the war. Even though the WFP Country Office had been attacked and at one point taken over, the food-distribution program had continued. It was now time to broaden the relief assistance and include other UN agencies, donor countries, and NGOs, all eager to join in the peace and recovery process.

As was customary in this type of relief operation, WFP and the United Nations High Commissioner for Refugees organized a UN interagency mission to assess the situation in various parts of the country. This time, however, we did not meet with warlords before our departure; the war was ostensibly over. Instead, we met with Ruth Perry, the woman who chaired an interim council made up of the five faction leaders who had been waging war in Liberia. The warlords accepted her because she was quite elderly, did not represent any particular group, and was not interested in the presidency. She wanted only to see an end to the senseless killing of innocent people and the destruction of Liberia.

Ruth Perry met with five of us at midday under a shelter jutting out from the main part of her house. Chickens scurried around us and under her Mercedes as we talked. She was concerned about the fragile peace and was embarking on a tour of the country to meet with the various chiefs and warlords, hoping to convince them to respect the peace accord and to join in the elections. It was agreed that another member of the assessment mission and I would travel with her to Zwedru, one of the larger towns in the northeastern county of Grand Geddah. In addition to meeting with the chiefs and townspeople, we would carry out a preliminary assessment of the relief needs in and around Zwedru.

Traveling to that area was only possible by helicopter. Most bridges had been destroyed, and the roads had not been maintained in seven years. Ruth Perry brought her Mercedes so that she would have an official vehicle to move from the airport to the center of the town. She flew in the smaller UNOMIL helicopter, while we went on board the larger ECOMOG (Economic Community of West Africa Military Observation Group) Russian-made MI-15 helicopter along with her armed ECOMOG escort and the Mercedes.

We landed first. Our security advisor, provided to ECO-MOG by a US security agency, told us to stay on board while he stepped out onto the landing field. He carried an automatic weapon and a pistol in a holster on his chest. He moved very quickly, looking side to side as he cautiously walked a short distance away from the helicopter. Then he motioned the ECOMOG soldiers to exit and take position around the helicopter. Once the safety perimeter was established around the aircraft, he waved to us to step down. Some of the ECOMOG soldiers accompanied us to a small building on the edge of the field. This small, one-room building used to be the Zwedru airport terminal.

The town was devastated. Most buildings had no roofs, and there were no stores, markets, schools, or hospital. Trees were growing inside the broken walls of houses. The streets were abandoned except for the occasional person heading for the church, one of the only buildings that was still intact. It was in this church that Ruth Perry met the townspeople who had returned to Zwedru and some of the ex-combatants. They started with a few songs and continued with speeches and discussion. Everyone was worried about the peace accord. Would they have a strong enough voice in a new government? Would they be treated fairly? Ruth Perry did her best to reassure them that the election would be free and fair. The onus was on them to get out and vote.

When we returned to the helicopter, I asked the security advisor why he had taken so many precautions as he stepped down from the helicopter.

"I arrived on a very different scene a few months earlier when I came to rescue a senior officer of the US Embassy who was being held hostage by General Ruth Antilla, the local warlord," he explained. "The first thing I saw when I arrived was one of the fighters walking by the helicopter carrying someone's leg over his shoulder. As I approached the small terminal, another fighter was roasting someone's testicles over an open fire. Antilla was holding the American up against the wall with a knife to his throat. We argued, then pleaded with her. We negotiated, and finally she let him go and told him to get the hell out of her area."

Our mission was the first visit to this area since that incident.

April 1999

Voinjama again, where I had been held hostage three years earlier. At dusk the town gradually came alive. I could hear the quiet bustle of people walking about, enjoying the cool air as the heat of the day subsided. The people were trying to return to their normal lives after the trauma of war. Some were setting up tables with small items for sale—cigarettes, edible roots and leaves, bush meat, toiletry articles. There was a stillness in the auburn air as the sun went down. No electricity, no running water. Oddly, I felt peaceful walking around the town, nostalgic for a time when villages were small and pleasures simple. No cars, no electricity, no music, no televisions, no wars.

We had been assured by the government of Liberia and the UN field security coordinator that the area was safe. I had been here on three occasions recently and there had been no problems. Voinjama was now a large staging area for bringing relief supplies to some forty thousand Sierra Leone refugees who were in camps in Kolahun and Vajun, which were on the border with Sierra Leone. Most of the food aid that was handled in Voinjama was for these refugees.

We had an evening meal with the local authorities, the assistant minister of planning, the executive director for Liberian reconstruction, Rehabilitation and Recovery Commission, and the Liberian government regional security advisor. Everybody was so pleased to welcome us. They kept repeating how much they appreciated the aid being provided by the UN and the donor governments. Members of the team remarked that they felt the whole evening very uplifting as we headed for bed in our respective guest houses at about eleven o'clock.

Around four o'clock in the morning we were awakened by gunfire somewhere in the distance. Then the shooting stopped. *Some soldiers have probably gotten drunk and are shooting in the air,* I thought. It grew quiet again as I listened to the sounds of crickets chirping away. Then I heard the sound of muffled voices on the road near the guest house. It was like the humming of bees. I thought that people were going early to the market. What I didn't know was that the townspeople were fleeing.

At five o'clock it started up again, but this time it was right outside the WFP compound. Within minutes we heard loud voices and the sound of an automatic weapon just outside the door. Armed men and boys barged in. I jumped out of bed, and as I stepped out into the corridor I came face to face with a gunman. He was like one of the many child soldiers I had seen before. No uniform, just a teenager with a big weapon.

"Give me small, small money and we go away," he said to me, as he pointed his assault rifle at my head.

Young "soldiers" in Liberia. (Paul Arès)

Thinking that these child soldiers just wanted to rob us, I offered Liberian dollars. No good. He threw them on the ground.

"You give dollars, US dollars," he said.

I gave him the $75 I had in my wallet.

"Now just leave the compound, leave us alone," I said.

But they had no intention of leaving us alone. Instead, they herded us into the front room of our guest house and demanded keys for all our vehicles. We were told to get into the cars, smaller pickups with open backs, and go with them to their command center. We drove the cars as they rode in the back. While we were driving, I remember going over in my mind the points I had read in a security document on what to do if you are a victim of a hostage-taking. I went over them methodically. *I just might need to guide us through what appears to be a worsening situation,* I kept thinking.

The streets were virtually empty except for the rebels, who we later learned were a group of disgruntled faction fighters. Like so many other child soldiers, they were kids between the ages of ten to early twenties and, like Pied Pipers, they attracted other children to their ranks as they moved through the town. We saw children with pieces of metal, machetes, knives, and sharpened sticks; utilitarian tools quickly fashioned into weapons. We saw villagers on their knees facing a wall with their hands tied behind their backs. Some had been beaten.

There was a great deal of confusion at the command center. The rebels were disagreeing among themselves. Many were unruly, some seemed to be drunk or drugged, while others were smoking marijuana. The younger fighters were not well armed, but the older boys had AK-47s and some had rocket-propelled grenades. They had been fighting with the rebels in Sierra Leone after the war in Liberia ended. Some had military fatigues, others were in tee-shirts, and a few had Liberian army uniforms stolen from the barracks that they had captured during the night. That was the shooting that I had heard at four o'clock. One of the older boys had a helmet and rode on the roof of a pickup, waving his AK-47 in the air. "Hey man, we fight again," he yelled, rejoicing at being back in battle.

After much arguing among themselves, it was decided that we would be taken back to the WFP compound in two vehicles so that we could collect our bags. I thought this a hopeful sign; perhaps they would allow us to leave. But I was wrong. Four of the rebels jumped onto the back of our truck, the lead vehicle, and we left for the compound. On the way another group of rebels appeared on the road, stopped us, and demanded the vehicles.

"Out of the way! Out of the way! We are taking these people back to their house," someone shouted from the back of our vehicle.

"No, man. These people stay here. We take the cars," yelled the group blocking the road. We stayed frozen to our seats. "We fire the car. Get out, or we fire [on] the car," they continued.

"Drive forward. Go!" yelled one of the gunmen on the back of our vehicle. He wanted to assert his authority over the group blocking the road. We were his captives.

Marcel Descombes, the head of our sub-office in Voinjama, was sitting in the driver's seat of my car.

"This is getting bad. I've seen this in Rwanda," he said. "When they start fighting among themselves, it gets very dangerous for us."

"You're right. This is getting out of hand," I replied.

At that moment one of the rebels jumped up and, sprawling in front of me on the hood of the car, pointed an AK-47 at my face through the glass.

"I goin' to fire [shoot] you," he yelled.

His eyes were drug glazed, without expression. I froze in my seat, thinking *This is it, my life is over.*

At that very moment, and to my great relief, another older fighter arrived on a motorbike. I had seen him at the command center. He seemed to have more authority. He gave the order to continue to the compound and all the others obeyed. What a reprieve. Once there, we were ordered to bring all our bags into the front room. A pillage began. Watches, alarm clocks, shortwave radios, and whatever money was in our pockets or shaving kits was taken away. I didn't have any money left in my wallet because of my earlier effort at getting the rebels to leave us alone.

"I have no more money. It was taken by your friends," I said, showing them my empty wallet.

This prompted a strange declaration from one of the rebels, perhaps to justify their action: "Charles Taylor is murdering innocent children. He is oppressing the people of Liberia. Those who oppose him are in prison. We are tired of fighting in Sierra Leone. We want Liberia back."

It was just after 11 a.m. Our ordeal had been going on since 5 a.m., yet we had to stay alert. Then we heard shooting as the security forces of the Liberian Army began a counter attack to repulse the rebels. Since the WFP guest house was on the southern edge of town, this is where it began. We all dove for the floor as the rebels took up positions on each side of the guest house. We were in the middle of the firefight, the crackle of machine-gun fire surrounded the compound. I could also feel the burst of a larger weapon being fired right outside the window. It was as if I were pulling the trigger myself.

I looked around to see how my colleagues were doing. Everybody was cringing on the floor. We couldn't talk. We couldn't move. My thoughts drifted: *What am I doing here? How did we get caught up in this mess? I hope nobody gets hurt. How painful it would be for our families if we got killed. What would it be like to get shot? How would it feel?*

Then the fighting stopped and the rebels came back into the house and ordered us, at gunpoint, into the vehicles. We didn't know what they planned to do with us. Use us as human shields? Take us into the bush and hold us indefinitely?

The rebels took us back to their command center, but the fighting got too heavy, so they moved us to the CRS building a short distance away. It wasn't long before bullets were flying in our direction again. Hastily, we were herded to the hospital building next door.

"You will be more protected inside the hospital," one of our captors said. They were trying to protect us. That sounded like good news.

Bullets hit the walls of the hospital. Crack! Crack! We

rushed toward an innermost room for more protection. It was dark and crowded with Liberians taking refuge from the fighting. These Liberians, members of the Loma ethnic group, were also being chased by the rebels. Liberia had recently come out of seven years of war, and they had just come back home to Voinjama full of hope. And now the fighting was starting up again.

I can still hear a little girl crying, and her mother trying to comfort her. I listened, then there was silence, and then it was the mother who started weeping. Such a deep, sorrowful sound.

Oh, God. How this hurts, I thought to myself.

Every now and then a bullet would strike the walls. The walls trembled, dust and plaster fell as a mortar shell exploded right next to the hospital. There was real panic as there was nowhere else to go. One could only hope that the next shell would not come through the roof.

A wounded rebel was brought to one of the adjacent rooms. I was told that he was the one who had spoken to us back at the guest house.

Poor kid, I thought. *He said that he was prepared to die for his cause. He probably will. There is very little anyone can do for him here.* He died a short while later.

I kept watching the others in our group. They were all very quiet. Everybody was absorbed in his or her thoughts, staring straight ahead. Waiting and hoping that somehow it would all end and we would be fine.

The group of expatriates in the hospital increased slightly— the eight of us who had been taken hostage earlier in the morning had been joined in the hospital by an American woman working for the Carter Center and a Swedish national working for a medical NGO. Some national officers also came with them, including a wounded driver.

Explosions, then tense silence, my mind moving ahead to what might happen next. Down the hall, a tall, muscular gun-

A young woman holds her baby, standing in a refugee camp in the town of Bong Mines, Liberia. (UNICEF/95-0206/Giacomo Pirozzi)

man with an AK-47, stripped naked to his belt, a red bandana around his head, pushed his way toward us.

This guy thinks he's Rambo, I thought. *He certainly looks the part.*

All the Liberians scurried out of his way; obviously not a guy to mess with.

Then I got worried. I was trembling, and I couldn't control it, thinking once again: *This is it. This is the end of my life.* In my mind I was preparing to take a bullet in the chest. I wondered what it would feel like.

"I am with the security forces of Liberia. You are free to go now," he said, and then he was gone.

My nightmare plays this one out differently. This fighter is actually the executioner and kills us all.

THE NEXT DAY we were evacuated by helicopter to Monrovia and then later to the Ivory Coast. We arrived in Abidjan near-ly two days later at ten o'clock in the morning. It was a tremendous relief to find my wife, Linda, and friends waiting for me at the airport. I was able to let go of my emotions for a moment as I held Linda in my arms. It had been very trau-matic for her, also. Like other wives and husbands, she had lived through terrible moments not knowing if we would come out of Liberia dead or alive.

Linda has always stood by waiting for me as I went in and out of these conflict areas. She has been steadfast in her determination to share with me the highs, the lows, and the stressful moments. Although I did not always tell her about some of the risks that I had taken in doing my work, so that she would not get overly worried, she knew that doing this work was not easy and that there was some element of risk. The times that I did share some of the more difficult moments, she was strong. Always, she clung to the belief that I knew where the fine line was, that I would not cross it. Things had gone wrong on this trip, the unexpected had hap-pened.

From the airport we went home and spent a few hours talking. We focused on being very thankful that we were both fine and that other members of the hostage group also seemed to be all right. It was so good to be back in Abidjan, to see normal activity in the streets, and to talk to friends. We decided that we would do what was most relaxing for us: play a round of golf with our closest friends. It would help get our minds off the ordeal we had both just been through. It would help us regain a sense of normalcy.

Usually, we would play golf on weekends toward the end of the afternoon when there was always a breeze coming off the ocean. On this day that breeze felt particularly soothing. I walked with my arms stretched out, just feeling that soft, gentle wind and thinking how great it was to be alive. I felt as if I could just float on air. There are times now when I will just reach out in the open air, feel the wind, and that sensation of sweet freedom comes back over and over again.

TODAY THE STORM of memory after the hostage experience seems to be subsiding, to be passing. Light and calm return. I continue working. I do this type of work because I believe in what we are trying to achieve and experience a tremendous sense of satisfaction when I help people. I see severely malnourished children on one trip, and when I return a month later, they are running around and smiling. But my approach to my work, and my role as a manager, has changed. In the past I never liked losing control of my emotions, and I shut myself down in order to do the work. I know this is not possible anymore.

Sometimes it's a simple image of someone suffering a tremendous loss, relief after an ordeal, or sharing in the thought of someone's grief that will quickly bring my emotions to the surface, where they belong.

9 *Behind the Lines*
Sierra Leone

David Snyder

"I have heard aid workers offer days like this when people ask why they do what they do—the visible impact of handing someone some food or a plastic tarp to keep the rain off. It's tangible, certainly, rewarding for the immediacy it offers to both recipient and provider."

Sierra Leone, August 1999

Though some who have been here might disagree—and some will—Sierra Leone feels evil to me. Not cold sweat, nightmare evil. I've never known that, and I hope I never will. Rather, it whispers, swirls in street-corner conversations, or shuffles by on crutches. A stump where a hand has been, a head without ears, a face without lips.

I'm not prepared for what the war has done here. I know academically, of course; I've read the UN report ranking Sierra Leone as the most disadvantaged nation in Africa, a country where a forty-six-year-old man is, statistically, cheating death. But before today the closest I've really come to understanding is during my conversations with Jacques Montouroy, the Catholic Relief Services (CRS) staff member with whom I am traveling to Lunsar. I've known of him since my first days with the agency. Passionate and outspoken, built like a rugby player, Jacques has seen many of the world's nightmares in his thirty years in the field. He's been shot at during a coup in Haiti and, on his first night in Angola, was confronted in his house by a knife-wielding burglar. Jacques responded by breaking a radio over the man's head.

A group of adult amputees, victims of rebel attacks in the eastern part of Sierra Leone, rest at the Waterloo camp for displaced persons near Freetown. (UNICEF/HQ98-0323/Robert Grossman)

"War? What war?" Jacques spits when I ask about the effects of the war on the people of Lunsar. "It's a bloody mess, not a war."

A mess, certainly, but also an almost palpable sensation. I felt it first in Freetown when I saw the mutilated victims–the young girl in a brilliant red button-up dress, her right leg ending in a knotted stump just above the ankle. Standing with Jacques on the balcony of the CRS office overlooking the city, he points out a badly patched bullet hole in the office wall, the shot that killed a night guard during a Revolutionary United Front (RUF) rebel attack years earlier. Though alive with the remarkable vitality of its people, smiling from the shops and markets that line its dirty streets, Freetown seems claustrophobic to me, overcrowded with those who fled the countryside and the memories they brought with them. The city itself seems cornered, pinned against the Atlantic by the hills pressing in around it.

Then, on the road to Lunsar, I feel it again, this evil. We're on a muddy track rutted by the heavy trucks ahead of us, a food convoy heading east toward rebel lines. The route is broken by the checkpoints of the Economic Community of West African States Monitoring Group (ECOMOG) soldiers, laconic, malarial Nigerians who peer half-heartedly into our Land Cruiser before waving us on after a few perfunctory questions. They're here as a peacekeeping force, though with the country still volatile there is precious little peace to keep. Jacques is calm, blending a polished checkpoint demeanor of courtesy and self-assurance. And though the ECOMOG soldiers inspire neither fear nor confidence—or perhaps because of it—I feel uneasy. Last month thirty-six UN observers and aid workers were abducted by the RUF in the eastern part of the country. There is now an official ceasefire, but each checkpoint we pass is another knot in the rope back to Freetown slipping from our hands.

I crack the seal on a bottle of warm mineral water and ask Jacques about his time in Liberia, where he'd gone in 1990 to help set up a relief program for those displaced by that country's civil war. He begins dismissively, as he often does, but the story takes shape as the memories resurface. With rebels and government soldiers exchanging fire in the streets of Monrovia, Jacques says, he had been asked by a US Embassy doctor to drive two wounded civilians to the hospital. He agreed, but on his way back had come across Prince Johnson, one of the rebel leaders then fighting to overthrow the Liberian government. Jacques was immediately arrested and handcuffed to a young Liberian, seconds before Johnson fired a burst from his AK-47 into the man's stomach. Jacques had shown me a photo of the moment, captured by an AP photographer and run in newspapers around the world. It shows the young Liberian flat on his back, his eyes rolling back in his head and his right hand hovering limply over his abdomen. Jacques is reaching out toward Johnson with his left hand, beseeching him not to shoot the man again. Ignoring Jacques's pleas, Johnson stepped up and fired another burst, killing the man instantly.

"It was all planned, a big stunt," Jacques says. "The man he killed was his own driver. He even put a Red Cross bib on the guy to make it look like he was killing a relief worker."

Though detained overnight, Jacques was released unharmed the next morning and sent on with a message from Johnson that nobody in Liberia was beyond his reach. Jacques was picked up by US Marines later the same day and evacuated from the country.

With this story in my head we pass the last ECOMOG checkpoint, marked with a red rag on a stick. I'm hoping Jacques's luck still holds. Several miles further on, there's a log dragged across the road. And there they are, the RUF rebels: four teenagers slouched beneath the fronds of a banana tree.

A few words are exchanged between the group members as we roll to a stop, and they shuffle to their feet. The tallest, wearing a faded pair of fatigue pants, a Michael Jordan tank top, and a baseball cap turned backward, could be a kid anywhere. Despite the heavy early morning clouds of the rainy season, he is wearing an oversized pair of dark sunglasses that obscure most of his skinny face. He looks us over for a few seconds and introduces himself as Major Alfred. He is no older than nineteen.

Jacques begins the explanation that is to see us through the next dozen checkpoints: We are with CRS, following the

David Snyder in Bera Dibele, a small port town on the Sunkuru River, Congo. (Courtesy David Snyder)

food convoy whose safe passage has been guaranteed by both the government and the local RUF commander. With a slight flurry of impatience, Jacques presents the authorization letter granting us permission to travel the route.

To the right, leaning against the wall of a small mud house thirty yards off the road, three young men are watching us. Like the others at the checkpoint, they are all wearing sunglasses. One has on a pink woman's blouse, and another has a black leather beret perched shapelessly on his head. Chalked on the wall above them in eerily juvenile print are two large-lettered lines of graffiti. "RUF is here," and, "This time, no joke–by Col. Paul."

Major Alfred pauses for a long moment beside the car before handing the letter back to Jacques, unfolded. Every gesture seems an overemphasis of his authority. Finally, he nods to the other teens and the log is dragged slowly aside. We grind on through the mud, repeating the same exchange at each checkpoint until, just after 9 a.m., we reach Lunsar.

Several hundred people are waiting for the food distribution at a Catholic school in the town. The morning is already uncomfortably hot. Many of those milling about are carrying umbrellas against the hazy sun that is just beginning to fight through the humidity. I notice an old man wearing a wool blazer and, just outside the gate, a woman in a bright yellow ankle-length raincoat, the kind that school crossing guards wear on wet fall days back in my hometown. It seems another world. I'm sweating through my tee-shirt as we pull into the compound.

Inside, Jacques immediately wades into unloading the six trucks of our convoy. As I'm gathering my things from the back seat of the Land Cruiser, a short, bearded man appears beside me and introduces himself. His name is Father Gianni, an Italian priest who had been a teacher at the school until it was looted four months ago by the RUF. Before that, he says, the school boasted the finest physics and chemistry labs in Sierra Leone, offering twenty scholarships a year for local students to go to college. "It makes me sick to come here now," he says, as we crunch through broken test tubes littering the ground. Angry graffiti covers the walls and chalkboards, and the heavy wooden desks are scarred by machete blows. Dozen of computers have been smashed–a senseless waste. Next door, the auto repair shop is empty, its tools stolen.

Miraculously, what we need for the food distribution is intact–a warehouse for the wheat and controlled access to the site through two black iron gates in the perimeter wall of the compound. By 11:30 a.m., the distribution is under way.

Armed young men of the RUF move around inside the compound. They are here, they say, to provide security. Most just linger. Others move along the lines of people forming up outside of the gate, threatening them into rigid formation with thin eucalyptus branches. They remind me of the menacing Macedonian soldiers I'd seen four months earlier at the Blace border crossing. To escape their attention, four of us had driven up into the hills above the town with boxes of high-energy biscuits for the refugees crossing the mountains from Kosovo. The soldiers caught up with us a few minutes later and began chasing away those gathering around the vehicle, then threatened us off the hill.

Jacques's patience with the constant harassment of the

As armed soldiers stand nearby, a group of women, many with malnourished babies in their laps, sit on benches at a feeding center run by Action Internationale Contre la Faim and Médecins Sans Frontières near the southern city of Bo, Sierra Leone. (UNICEF/HQ95-0950/Robert Grossman)

RUF is wearing thin. He quarrels loudly with several of the young men by the front gate, and I laugh to myself at the thought of him breaking a radio over someone's head. But it's a temporary pleasure. My patience is thinning, too. Standing outside of the gate, I see a young girl waiting in line with her mother. Slipping the camera from my shoulder, I make eye contact with them and smile. Though the young girl turns her face away, her mother smiles back self-consciously. I approach and raise my camera, but before I take the photo a rebel in a dirty white shirt rushes into view and begins swatting at the group with a branch. An argument erupts and spreads quickly to two nearby lines. I lower the camera and walk away.

A few yards down I notice a rebel standing by himself, his back to the low concrete wall of the compound. Short and broad shouldered, he is wearing a dark blue coverall worn white at the knees and a floppy, full-brimmed hat like the kind they give away free at sporting events. There is nothing particularly striking about him, except that he is alone, disinterested in either the distribution or the company of the other young men. He stands impassively as I approach and acknowledges my presence by shifting his weight to the foot furthest from me. I notice that the squat, rust-flaked barrel of his AK-47 is packed tightly with dry mud, and I think, absurdly, how dangerous that will be when it's fired. But standing next to him I feel suddenly foolish, wiping my forehead with a red handkerchief and trying to open a conversation in some way that doesn't sound ridiculous. I can't think of anything to say. Casting a line, I hold up my camera and ask for a photo. He shakes his head. I ask his name, and he answers flatly, "Abraham." I offer mine. Silence again. I ask him how old he is: "Seventeen." How long has he been with the RUF? "Seven years." His answers come in empty whispers, and he offers nothing beyond what I ask for. I search his face for clues, an unconscious habit wherever language and culture tangle my ability to communicate. Is he angry with me? Embarrassed, even, by the attention? But there is no emotion in his eyes to guide me. There is absolutely nothing.

It is, in most respects, an unremarkable exchange. But I feel unsettled, and it takes me a minute to figure out why: it's what I see, or don't see, in his face. Trying again, I ask where his family lives.

"I have no family," he says. "They came and killed my mother and father and made me go with them. Now I don't want to fight anymore."

It is the only real insight he offers, but the lines dribble out in the same flat monotone. He speaks like a translator, formulating someone else's life into a language I can understand and awaiting my question in return. But I get only single words again after that, spoken through the same blank expression. Is he tired of fighting? "Yes." What will he do when the war is over? A shrug. I try for a while longer, but nothing else comes. Finally, I walk off.

But Abraham has given me the answer I can't find in his face, the reason, at least, for his emptiness. It isn't anger or fear, I think, but both–a numb self-defense against the memories of the last seven years. In the five minutes I spent with him, he seemed dead to me on a level far beyond indifference, at a depth from which I doubt he can ever resurface, certainly not if this war continues, probably not even if it ends.

But there's more, and it is not about him; it's about me. What bothers me most about Abraham is that I don't really know how to feel about him. I stand beside the concrete wall of the compound and watch him for several minutes, but I can't find a new category for him in my head. He is a victim, certainly, but that word is over-used. A casualty? In a way, I suppose. But he is also the nightmare that so many here are living with–the nightmare that once came for him. I can't untie him from the girl in the red dress in Freetown, from the hole in the office wall, from everything unnerving about this place. In the end, it's easier not to try to understand, easier to keep that distance between us.

By 4:30 p.m. the distribution is over. Leaning against the Land Cruiser, I swallow the last of my water and watch a young man collecting his ration of beans in a brightly colored square of cloth. He folds each corner carefully and ties the package in a tight bundle, then gathers up a half-bag of wheat in the crook of his left arm and moves slowly toward the gate.

I have heard aid workers offer days like this when people ask why they do what they do–the visible impact of handing someone some food or a plastic tarp to keep the rain off. It's tangible, certainly, rewarding for the immediacy it offers to both recipient and provider. There are few such pure exchanges in life. But for me it's an anticlimax as well, the emptiness of a compound that has been thriving all day, the sudden absence of color and sound. It's like the odd hollowness of coming home after traveling, the feeling you get when your last guest leaves.

Three rebels approach and, seeing my camera, ask for a photo. I'm tired of them, tired of taking their photos. I ready the camera reluctantly. One of the three slides a pistol from the waistline of his dirty jeans. They all pose, stone faced, and place their hands on the weapon like a team with a trophy.

Three rebels ask for a photo.
(David Snyder)

10 *What Is Beautiful* Afghanistan

Marleen Deerenberg

"I want to assist people in changing their environment, changing their lives, in order to improve their chances of survival in this world gone crazy."

In the evenings, in the small bedroom of a cheap and dirty hotel in Peshawar, Pakistan, my boyfriend Hugo and I talk about the future. It is 1993 and we have both recently graduated from college. We are traveling, experiencing other cultures. Holland annoys me: our snug and petty lives there, our easy political correctness, our circle of friends who all think and feel the same about everything. Should we have a child? We know other couples who already have children. When I visit them and see their worn-out faces or hear about their daily concerns I don't envy them. So we have decided, Hugo and I, to apply for a job with a medical relief organization, and we expect to be posted to a mission soon. Will we stay together? Will our life turn into one big holiday? No, surely not. There will be loads of work to do.

Summer 1995

After a year in Albania with Hugo, I am on my way to Afghanistan alone. Hugo is ready to return to Holland, but I am not, and ask for another posting, a short one. Hugo will wait for me, he says.

Taza Gul, my driver, is smiling politely and offering me music; I can play any cassette I like. Our car is loaded with computer spare parts, a repaired photocopy machine, and

Marleen Deerenberg on the right with two local colleagues in the summer of 1999. In the background, a lake near Kabul where, in peacetime, locals gather for picnics and swimming. (Courtesy Marleen Deerenberg)

boxes of medicine. The rugged pickup behind us is carrying armed men. This escort car was arranged on the Pakistani border. For security reasons my driver is not allowed to take expatriates outside the city without the protection of armed guards. So many factions are active in the area, all maintaining their own fighting force, that the roads here are as unsafe as any medieval route in Europe, packed with bandits, robbers, and hijackers. As it's one of the principles of Médecins Sans Frontières (MSF) not to carry armed persons in our vehicles, we make sure the armed men follow us in a rented car.

After the marvels of the Khyber Pass, wriggling its way through the bare mountain peaks, my first impression of the Afghan landscape is a bit disappointing. We lurch through a broad valley flanked by gray mountain ranges, a small river flowing far away on one side. The road is full of holes; the soil as far as I can see seems to consist of pure rocks and sand; the rare building we pass is falling apart and marked with countless bullet holes. Only after a while do I get to see some green around me; for a long stretch the road is closely flanked by olive trees.

Desert again, nothing but yellowish dust, and in the middle of that suddenly the mud walls and beige tents that make up the refugee camp where MSF runs six clinics and three feeding centers. The clinics—whitewashed concrete boxes—are easy to recognize among the makeshift homes of the Kabuli people who sought refuge here after their city was shelled to pieces more than a year ago. Entering Jalalabad itself, the driver waves goodbye to the escort car and we find our way through the bustling mazes of the city on our own. I see palm trees towering above the gates in the mud walls, I hear carpet sellers, I smell the fuel stations, wooden sheds loaded with jerrycans full of diesel. There's hardly a man without a beard and no woman without a burqa on the streets.

We stop in front of a blue gate, intricately decorated with metal patterns, and Taza Gul presses the klaxon. The face of a *chowkidor*–a guard–appears behind a spy hole, nods, and starts unbarring the gate. The metal doors swing open with a clamoring noise. This is my new home.

Each morning I feel as though I am living a fairy tale. I love to walk around in a long embroidered dress and baggy trousers, including the exotic scarf, that is considered correct dress for women. During the day I stroll through the office to perform my duties as an administrator and chat with the local employees. Young and old, the men are delighted in my company and seem all too willing to carry out any order or errand I ask of them. In the afternoons I take a translator with me to the bazaar and bargain for ethnic jewelry, let the henna painters decorate my fingers, and search for pillow covers decorated with mirrors in flowery patterns. Five times a day the mysterious call of the muezzin gives an oriental flavor to my hours. It is like a dream. In the evening the male expatriates in the house pay me the utmost attention, and with the satellite dish and the video recorder, the garden full of roses and a campfire going, we don't get bored. Even though it's chokingly hot, electricity is often not available, and the food provided by our local cook often tastes like burned rubber, I feel like a princess in a harem.

Still, I know, and feel, the darker, uglier, reality behind the walls of my palace: a child dies from dehydration, our engineer can't get the water piping scheme going as fast as he would like, and there's fraud going on in one of the clinics where the medicines are distributed. One of my colleagues at the camp has to sack his closest Afghan friend because of this. And when I have to visit the camp myself, I return to reality. I go there once a month to pay the clinic and feeding-center staff. We count the money beforehand, enormous piles of devalued Afghani notes, a big bundle for each person no matter how meager the salary. I take my two assistants and a big metal box with three locks on it into the Land Cruiser and set out for the camp. We are welcome guests and are always treated with awe.

I feel like a warlord.

What does a warlord do? He hands out life and economic security to many people. The people complain, of course. The wages are too low compared to other organizations, there aren't enough cookies, the workload is too heavy and we need to employ more people. They know the right person for the job, a distant relative. Perhaps we would like to meet him?

All I can do is listen and say I'll discuss your request with the project manager. As for the wages, I know we pay more or less the same as the other NGOs and the International Committee for the Red Cross (ICRC). The UN pays more; that's a fact.

In the midst of this conversation about money, I see them looking at my huge bracelets, my lapis lazuli earrings, my fancy dress. Most of our local employees have fled from Kabul and are now either staying in the camp or with relatives in Jalalabad. Some of them occupied quite high positions in the former regime, headed by the communist-oriented Najibullah. Their time is over, and they know it. Others made their career in the ranks of the mujahedin. Both factions in the office—former communists and mujahedin—are not on friendly terms and will do their best to malign each other's reputation in front of me. It's hard to get them to cooperate. I get the feeling there's a lot more going on than meets the eye, at least mine.

ONE DAY, close to the end of my first mission in Afghanistan, Taza Gul says he wants to marry me and live in Holland. I remind him that he is already married and has four children to feed.

"Keep your eyes on the road, if you don't mind," I say.

"Oh, Miss Marleen, please don't tell this to Mr. Patrick, please," he says.

Patrick is the project coordinator in Jalalabad, a bulky Irishman with a good sense of humor, very conscientious in his job. Does Taza Gul know I spend most of my nights in Jalalabad in Mr. Patrick's bed?

Winter 1996

The war in Afghanistan, which has never really abated, continues. The men in the office follow the Taliban advance in the south and west of the country by radio. Will the holy soldiers come and capture Jalalabad as well? And would we like that? Rumor has it that the religious students, once they occupy a certain area, thoroughly pacify it by collecting all arms available. Ajmal, my young assistant, tells me that he and his brothers take turns guarding their house at night. With a gun in their hands, they sit on the roof to make sure that no bandits enter to kidnap their teenage sisters.

I'm back in my house with the big garden, the campfire place, and the labyrinth of rooms for expatriates and guests. Holland seemed so dark and tiny by comparison, my job there so futile, my relationship stale. As soon as I heard of an opportunity to return to Afghanistan for six months, I made up my mind.

This time I am responsible for logistics as well as finance. I have a hard time talking about tuning radios and repairing broken diesel pumps. Irish Patrick has left but has been replaced in my affections by Idris, a tall and smooth Sudanese water engineer. We talk religion, philosophy, and physics in front of the fireplace in the living room or outside in the garden under the stars.

Our project has changed as more and more people are leaving the camp, which leaves us wondering what to do with the few that stay put. The UN chairs discussions on the topic. Should they cut the food rations to convince families to return to their hometown? Not yet is the conclusion; the war leaves many things insecure.

My two female colleagues and housemates, a nurse and a nutritionist, spend weeks sorting out the situation in the one feeding center we still run. A lot of cheating seems to have been going on. The nutritional biscuits that we distributed recently appear in shops in the camp bazaar and volunteers on our payroll, checking the tents for malnourished children and pregnant women, appear to have been favoring their own acquaintances with tokens for food. A midwife has to be

A woman and her toddler wait to be attended to at a therapeutic feeding center for displaced persons run by Médecins Sans Frontières on the outskirts of Herat, Afghanistan. (UNICEF/HQ00-0855/Roger LeMoyne)

employed to check whether the women who apply for extra food, claiming they are pregnant, are indeed in that condition. After a few days the midwife doesn't come to work; she has been threatened with violence by the beneficiaries.

Eventually, the team decides to close the feeding center and to keep only three of the five clinics open. The situation in the camp is tense, and we can hardly prevent a riot from breaking out. We have nightly discussions about the justification for keeping a presence in Jalalabad. We decide that Maud, a nurse-anthropologist, will set up an office in the Ministry of Health to organize training programs for traditional birth attendants in the surrounding villages and that the rest of our project will be dedicated to emergency preparedness.

As the war might reach Jalalabad, my main task becomes the checking of stocks: the chlorine, rehydration fluids and beds with holes in the middle of the matting for a possible cholera outbreak, the food, fuel and water in the bunkers, in the house, and in the office. I find out that my storekeeper is opening boxes of injectibles at the bottom, leaving the seals on top intact. The drugs disappear at night into the black market. Several guards and the head logistician must be involved.

THE COZIEST EVENING of the week is when Professor Wafiullah, our Pashtu teacher, comes around for a lesson. The whole team participates and we do our best to remember phrases like Ta dee kum za yee? Ze de Jalalabad jem (Where are you from? I'm from Jalalabad). Or, Ta de zma zrah sar yee aw de zma stergey turey yee (You are the head of my heart and the iris of my eye). The men in the office roar with laughter when I practice these phrases on them. The professor is so shy and peaceful a person, hesitant to criticize our efforts, that although we all love him, we surely don't get fluent in the local language.

Fall 1996

I read about the Taliban take-over of Kabul in Amsterdam, where I am living again. I see the picture of the tortured bodies of Najibullah and his brother dangling from a lamppost. I hear the first rumors about negotiations for a pipeline to pass through Afghan territory to transport oil from the Caspian out to the Indian Ocean.

When Patrick and Idris, by coincidence, visit me in Amsterdam at the same time, we discuss politics in a café. Has this been the secret inspiration for the ever-continuing Iranian, Pakistani, Saudi, Russian, and US interference with the Afghan civil war? Does all the chaos and suffering we've seen simply come down to this: a monopoly on the transport of Turkmen oil? Of course, there's the individual warlord and opium baron profiting from the present situation, but they would never be able to prolong their efforts without foreign support. Can the world be so cynical a place?

I say goodbye to Patrick at the airport. He's off to Somalia. And Idris? He tells me he will go where he's needed most, but there's a chance that might be Jalalabad again. He got a job offer for a higher position with a much better salary.

Spring 1997

I am in Afghanistan again. Because the Taliban captured Jalalabad, the road to Kabul is open and we can visit the capital at last. "It's beautiful here," I say softly, as I set myself on the passenger seat next to Idris, close the door, and fasten the seatbelt. He turns his head, his eyebrows raised, a cold look in his eyes, as if to say, What are you seeing here that is beautiful?

We drive through a former shopping street, all the once grand and majestic buildings bombed into fragile fragments of brick. A window frame, the setting of a door, a lonely wall, a partition wall cut in half. I can count the bricks; they lie piled up in a friendly, messy way. Men and boys sell oranges from handcarts, blankets wrapped around their shoulders against the cold. Red carpets for sale are laid out between the ruins, and a group of men in jumpers and overcoats stands laughing behind a scale, surrounded by bloody goat skulls.

Idris tries to make conversation, hanging from the car window. In stammering Dari, he asks about the repairs in the neighborhood: latrines, new plumbing, the clearing of landmines. The men answer his questions and offer him a cake made of poppy seeds glued together with honey. They point at me. I nod modestly, my eyes cast down, my hands folded in my lap.

The blue river, full of ice floes, reflects the snow-clad mountains on both sides. Mountain chains cut through the patterns of streets and continuously expose the most surprising panoramas. I tell Idris that I can imagine why the Kabuli people who fled to Jalalabad and Pakistan are not able to forget their hometown. He shakes his head. "Sweet, what the hell are you doing here?" he asks me. "If you didn't come here to make yourself useful, you should go home. This country is more than a mere setting for your adventures. It is inhabited, you know!"

"Sweet," I reply. "It's their setting as well. These people live through their adventures just the same as we do. They are more than the powerless, shapeless, and nameless beggars you make them!"

My eyes fill with tears and I'm grateful for the shadow that my chador provides. Idris calls himself a giver. Once his job is finished here, he will leave and not look back. What does this giver to humankind have to offer me?

I CAME BACK to Afghanistan to work with Healthnet International, a different NGO. The work now is more development than relief. The camps are nearly deserted, the displaced inhabitants returned to their homes in Kabul, so we are going to work in the poor villages in the remote mountainous areas. Using a network of local health volunteers, traditional birth attendants, and basic health centers, we will try to improve the living standard in the countryside. Different job, same house, and much the same colleagues. Taza Gul, my driver, for one. Even most of the expatriates are still around, including Idris and Maud. Ajmal, my former assistant, works for the ICRC now, but we keep in touch.

My Dutch adventure? That didn't work out really. Let's call it a half-year holiday. I feel my home is here, even though rough truths begin to surface. The cars, for instance. We have nine cars, most of them old hand-me-downs from MSF. When we need a new vehicle, we decide to buy it in Pakistan. On our one-year budget of US$1.5 million, an expense of US$40,000, 30 percent of which is tax, strikes me as extravagant. We want the project money to reach the destitute, and now it ends up in the pockets of Mr. Toyota and the notoriously corrupt Pakistani government.

All in all, it feels strange to be spending more than a million dollars a year. A big chunk goes to medicines, bought locally in Pakistan to cut down on freight costs. It's a headache to compare the prices of the products of different companies, as my assistant and I get confused by the drug names and brand names. We consult our medical coordinator for advice, and this takes time.

Another big beneficiary of our budget is Mr. Microsoft, as all our computers must be equipped with the customary software.

My own bank account shows an upward trend as all my expenses here are covered. I don't have a house in Holland anymore. No furniture, no appliances. My only earthly possessions are the clothes and tapes I brought with me to Afghanistan and some boxes of books in my parents' attic. Still, I've never felt so rich.

Life under the Taliban differs in certain ways from the

Mujahedin period. There are no weapons in civilian hands, a huge improvement. The members of my office staff don't have to defend their daughters and sisters from kidnapping any longer. For the women, however, new problems have arisen. The few schools for girls that existed before in the cities are ordered to close down, and female students are banned from universities. For a woman to walk in the streets without the cover of a burqa becomes a dangerous business. The religious fanatics proclaim the discrimination of women official policy, and the world starts to pay attention.

In the villages the change seems mainly for the good, at least in the Pashtun districts where we are working. In these remote areas men and women have inhabited separate worlds for ages, and because the Taliban know this, they hardly harass the villagers. People start to plow their fields again, although their most profitable crop remains poppy. The UN calls meeting after meeting to wreak havoc on the opium production. If a project tackles poppy cultivation, it's a sure way to get funded these days. I worry about the poor Afghans who rely on this crop for their livelihood. The main concern of the Western world is the situation in the Western world, and this opium is a nuisance, isn't it?

We hear about the first executions in the Kabul sports stadium: hand cutting for theft, stoning for adultery, the toppling of a wall over two homosexuals. Meanwhile, in Jalalabad, we try to cooperate with the twenty-five-year-old mullah who chairs the Ministry of Health. Our project manager, a highly cultured Sudanese surgeon, sprinkles their long afternoon conversations around the teapot with quotes from the Qur'an in an effort to convince the rigid-minded boy that the Holy Book supplies enough clues to promote the well-being and emancipation of women, without confinement. Slowly, very slowly, during the course of the coming years, there will be some progress there.

It is this same young minister who drives me nuts with requests to use the Land Cruiser we have assigned to the women doctors and midwives in the mother and child-care unit. We need this car to transport these health-care workers around the area; it's one of the core activities of our project. We are one of the only NGOs remaining here that continues to work for and with women. The local people cannot refuse the minister's requests, but I can, though it would not be diplomatic to refuse him all the time and risk our women workers or the cancellation of my visa, which must be renewed every three months.

Smuggling alcohol into the country has become dangerous, too, especially for the driver involved. I don't particularly fancy Taza Gul getting a beating for trying to help me sustain my addiction, so we get to live a mostly quiet and sober life. Idris is a Muslim himself, so he's happy with the change, but Maud and I escape sometimes to the American Club in Peshawar, Pakistan, where the Christian waiters serve a nasty white wine. It is on these excursions out of the country that self-doubts begin to surface: What are we trying to establish here, in a country so alien to us? How far do we want to go collaborating with an oppressive regime? What about our future? Our love affairs? Apart from the occasional one-night stand, Maud has been on her own for most of her life and hasn't met the man of her dreams as yet. And me, stuck with handsome Idris, who's got another girlfriend at home. What's going to happen when our party's over? I do fancy sweet Ajmal, not my employee anymore; he is desperately in love with me. But what's the risk involved in dating an Afghan under the nose of the Taliban?

Summer 1998

I would desperately like to get back into the country, but due to severe political unrest I've been evacuated to Pakistan. On August 7, two bombs blew up the US embassies in Kenya and Tanzania. Sympathizers of the fundamentalist Osama Bin Laden, a Saudi dissident hiding inside Afghanistan, claimed responsibility. On August 8, the Taliban captured Mazar-I-Sherif, the northern stronghold, and massacred thousands of people from other ethnic groups there. On August 20, the United States launched an attack with cruise missiles on training camps of Bin Laden's people, close to Jalalabad. As these places are well hidden and not easy to reach, I've never known their location.

We expats are already out of the country when the US attack takes place, because we've been warned in advance by the US State Department that terrorist groups are planning to kill a project manager. I worry what our Afghan friends and co-workers will think of us as we leave them behind as soon as we know there's trouble coming. What kind of solidarity is that? There's also the threat of a war between Iran and Afghanistan; the Taliban killed eleven Iranian diplomats when they took over Mazar-I-Sherif and more than seventy thousand Iranian soldiers are positioned along the border. Who knows what might happen in the region?

I spend my time reading the books former expats left behind in the guest house in Peshawar. *The Lord of the Rings* helps me pass some hours, and then there's Sartre and Nietzsche to dig into. Idris likes to watch the news several times a day. Bin Laden and Lewinsky become very familiar names. In the evenings we watch every videotape available in the local shops. Idris likes me to read to him, especially spy stories. I start to feel a bit paranoid myself.

"Whom of the expats here do you think is a spy?" Idris asks me one day.

"Nobody, of course," I say. I cannot imagine anybody being stupid enough to pose as a relief worker while helping to sustain a war.

"'Don't be so sure," Idris says, in his soft sweet voice.

'Think of the French guy we know, working only in Massoud's area. Think of your own boss, a Sudanese working closely with the Taliban. Think of my German colleague, who speaks the local languages fluently. Who knows what their real motives are to keep hanging around in a place like this?"

He must be joking, I think. I trust these people. If I really must imagine someone being a secret spy, my likeliest guess would be Idris himself. He's the one who always keeps his options open, announcing his departure then deciding to extend his contract again, receiving no personal mail, no visitors. But no. I can't believe it. For which government would he be spying? None of them would be worth it. And then a ridiculous thought strikes me: Others may think I am a spy! I've been in Afghanistan for more than three years. Why on earth am I still here? Is it because of Idris? Is it because I'm afraid to go home?

Ajmal, my former assistant, with whom I spent a short but romantic holiday in Pakistan last year, has fled the country. As a Tadjik, he felt the pressure from the Taliban getting stronger. After a period in Russia, he managed to reach Holland. He writes me lovely letters. He, who'd never before seen the sea, is walking the beach now, wet from Dutch rain. He shaved his beard and wears jeans instead of a shalwar qameez. Next time I fly to Holland, I decide, I'll pay him a visit.

At regular intervals people from Jalalabad travel up and down to Peshawar to brief us on the ongoing project activities and to take resources back with them. Waheed, my financial assistant, comes around to close the July books and collect some extra money so the salaries for August can be paid on time. The following week I hear he stole away from Jalalabad at night, taking all the salaries with him. I remember the discussion last year, when I decided to employ this man. The other Afghans in the office warned me that it was dangerous to give him so much responsibility, taking into account that he was from another part

Afghani mother and child. (UNHCR/P. Benatar)

of the country and had no relatives around Jalalabad. I perceived this resistance as clan politics and suspected that my staff wanted to see one of their own relatives employed instead of this poor stranger. But now I know I was wrong.

Even before the evacuation this has been a tough summer. The body of Professor Wafiullah, our old teacher, was dragged from the Kabul River, close to one of our health centers. He had been blindfolded, his hands tied behind his back. He and a colleague had been standing by the side of the road, waiting for the bus to the city, when a car full of armed men stopped by and forced them to get inside. Nobody knows whether these killers were Taliban or bandits. Rumor has it that the professor was a Christian. I find that hard to believe. During the years that I knew this man, he never gave me any reason to think he was not the most pious of Muslims. Others say he was murdered because he had a job with the UN, and others again think the crime had to do with the fact that he didn't want to vacate his house on the university compound when the Taliban wanted to take it over. A last possibility is that the main target of the murderers was not the friendly and modest professor but his younger and more militant colleague, who might have been involved in a secret opposition movement. Anyhow, both of them received the same treatment. I'll never know the truth, I guess, but I feel baffled that of all the Afghans I got to know over the years, this most peaceful and innocent person had to die this way.

BY THE END of September we are one of the first NGOs to send its expats back into Afghanistan. The UN, always strict on security, has withdrawn its workers and puts pressure on expats from other organizations not to return. We ignore its warnings and go on with our work in the villages where more and more men and women get trained in basic health care, hygiene, and prevention. Fields are plowed, new houses and shops are being built, and some schools start running again, although they are still only for boys and the curriculum is limited to religious topics.

While Afghanistan and the Taliban get more and more bad publicity, we continue our struggle for cooperation. "Tolerance for intolerance" is the way the director of our organization describes our purpose here during a visit. Now that I can see the progress we've made over the years, slowly, but in pace with the mental change in the minds of the rural people, I get more and more enthusiastic about the work itself. I don't want to bring relief, wait for shit to happen, and afterward bandage the wounded. I want to assist people in changing their environment, changing their lives, in order to improve their chances of survival in this world gone crazy.

When I join my Afghan and Sudanese colleagues in the rituals of Ramadan—the month of fasting—I feel happy and at ease. In the evenings, while feasting on dates and sweet pastries in front of the fire in the hearth, the Sudanese tell me more about their religion. For all of them it seems like a force, an inspiration, to help them sacrifice personal dreams and wishes for a greater good. It doesn't seem so different from the Christian blend of socialism my parents believe in or from the books about Buddhism I studied years ago. Although the history of Afghanistan seems to contradict this, I even see many similarities between Islam and communism.

"Why don't you become a Muslim too?" Idris often asks me. "That would make it easier for me to take our relationship seriously."

"How can I pretend to believe in something when I don't? I can't surrender to some Bigger Entity. I feel that my free and questioning mind is my main identity, and I cannot imagine ever giving that up."

"That's blasphemy of the worst kind, my sweet," Idris says and sadly shakes his head before he kisses me.

Summer 1999

I hear about droughts, ethnic cleansing, and the ongoing military struggle in the northeast of the country. There are more and more rumors about Bin Laden and his Arab fighters gaining strength inside the Taliban movement. Although it's been reported that Osama himself dwells in Jalalabad, we never see him on the streets. I do encounter more and more Arabs, though, young armed men huddled in the backs of pickups, who start sulking whenever they see my uncovered face.

In the countryside we're still involved in development and keep trying to convince people to start thinking again of building a future for themselves inside the country rather than escaping to the West. It's hard for them to trust anybody: their village elders, the government, or the aid community.

In Jalalabad people are pessimistic. All the young Afghans seem to have fled, and the office is full of gray-bearded men. Only one handsome and charismatic doctor–Zaher–stayed behind. He travels around the villages to convince the elders that our training programs will benefit their people. His wife and children live in Peshawar, so he has to sleep in a boarding room in our staff house during the week. He's an inspiring person and I admire his dedication to his work. However, he's trying to get accepted for a master's course in health management in Holland, so we're going to lose him as well.

At last we get the prolongation funding from the European Union (EU) for our main project. Normally, we should have smoothly run from one budget into the other, since the donor had agreed beforehand to keep funding our program for five years. After the first year, though, the EU suffered severe internal problems and all proposals were put on hold. For one and a half years we survived by scraping small amounts of money from here and there, shifted staff from the main project to another one, and paused several of our projects. As an administrator, it has been a challenge to bridge this period without sacking anybody. That I succeeded is a source for considerable pride.

Idris has left for another mission, though he told me he might be coming back. With him gone and my other colleagues living with their families, I stay mostly alone in the big house, sweating under the buzzing fans. I sit in the garden, study the palm trees and the roses, take care of a wild cat and her kittens, and contemplate my life. Will I be the last one left, staying here forever in this house full of memories? It feels as though I am preparing for my own funeral. But it's not easy for the organization to find a successor, because most people are not keen to work in a place so completely stripped of entertainment. Should I sacrifice my personal happiness for the greater good?

As far as the work is concerned, I feel content enough. Even if things will not work out in the end, we base our actions on good intentions. I like the way we try to reason backward to untangle the network of corruption, prejudice, and paternalism that so easily leads a well-meant initiative astray. How to make sure we reach the most needy? How to make sure we really get to hear their voice and help them gain more influence in local politics? And how to make sure the local politics has any impact at all in a country so sucked into the great game of world politics?

The Afghan women working for the project all pity me. I'm thirty-four years old, elderly, expired, because I haven't managed to get married and have a son. One of the midwives offers me her eldest son for marriage, a guy no more than nineteen years old. "You could stay here," she says, and I take it as a compliment.

I visit the project sites as much as possible, and I stay overnight in the houses of our midwives in many different villages. They are not from this area; all of them come from either Kabul or Jalalabad, where they finished their studies and would have preferred to stay and work. The ones from Kabul had to flee during the shelling in 1994; the ones from Jalalabad can't find any work there. We lured them to these remote mountain villages, which never before accommodated such highly educated women, by handing out jobs to their husbands as well, and by convincing the village leaders to provide them with houses, wood, and kerosene.

Even though I feel more involved than ever in the work itself, the loneliness in my private life depresses me. I discover my cat, my only companion, sitting trembling in the garden one day, her tail burned to ashes by playing children. Normal Afghan stray cats are wiser than to risk coming too close to human beings. I must have spoiled her, made her too trustful. Now and then I talk by phone to young Ajmal, living in a refugee center in Holland. He would like me to become his girlfriend again. Sweet, handsome Ajmal. What would it be like to meet on the beach?

I decide that this will really be my last summer here and make arrangements to start a study in September: a course in creative writing. That's what I missed most during all these years abroad: the artistic and intellectual climate that challenges the mind and provokes creative energy. To talk about fiction as if it's something that matters just as much, or maybe even more, than the daily economic struggle for life. It makes me feel guilty, because I do have a choice when so many others don't, but this time I go home. When I make my goodbye speech to the men of the project, I focus on the fact that although in many areas they face scarcity and shortages, at least they do have a job to be proud of. When I make my goodbye speech to the women, at another day and another location, I start to cry. Once back in Holland, it's questionable whether I will be able to find work as inspiring as this.

11 *The House of Prayer and Peace*
Sudan

Theresa Baldini, M.M.

We feel a little like Sarah and Abraham,
Living in South Sudan.
Planning a place of prayer and peace,
Where war is scarring the land.

Our house of prayer and peace is in the village of Narus, South Sudan. Sister Madeline McHugh and I are Contemplative Maryknoll Sisters. We are here to provide respite for the people displaced by the war between the Islamic North and the mostly Christian South. In 1983, the government in Khartoum introduced Sharia-Islamic law. This triggered the war, causing horrific suffering among the people.

Our presence here is a quiet, nonviolent, and modest one. It began in January 1986 and continued until 1992, was suspended for eight years, and began again in January 2000, by which time Sister Madeline, fully recovered from a deadly form of cerebral malaria, was seventy-nine years young, and I was sixty-three.

We have a friendship with the people around us. They see us doing our own cleaning, cooking, and gardening, and they help us expand our new metal dwelling, which has replaced the mud-and-grass *tukul* (hut) we lived in when we first moved here. Recently, with the help of our neighbors, we have added a small chapel, a *choo* (toilet), a shower, and a storeroom. A school for girls meets under the trees, and there is also a clinic in the compound staffed by two Ugandan sister-nurses.

Occasionally, we hire someone to help us pull up weeds

Maryknoll Sisters Madeline McHugh (on the left) and Theresa Baldini (on the right) in front of their house in Sudan. (Maryknoll Archives)

from our grounds. One young man planted four seedling papaya trees, which should bear fruit in about five years. What is five years in a war that has been going on for nearly twenty?

Many people have suffered in Sudan; more than two million have died since the war began. The land is decimated—there is nothing to buy in Narus—and the cynical leaders in Khartoum only have interest in power and oil, so the war continues, and worsens. The money from the oil—sold to

China, Sweden, The Netherlands, Malaysia, Canada, and other countries–perpetuates the war; military equipment is bought with the proceeds. Families are uprooted, moving from one place to another to find safety where little can be found. And a guerilla group, the Ugandan Lord's Resistance Army (LRA), paid by the Khartoum government to cause trouble in South Sudan, has been ruthlessly invading villages in our Diocese of Torit. Recently, over five hundred innocent civilians were slaughtered by the LRA. The people were having a funeral rite for someone who had died that day. The soldiers surrounded the group, made some of the villagers cut up the dead body, and forced them to eat the body. Afterward, everyone else was killed and mutilated, except for two who escaped.

We built our tin-roofed chapel in the midst of this war zone. Orange blossoms cascade into the front yard, exuding fragrance and life. We know we cannot solve the problems here, but we can listen with compassion and provide comfort. We communicate in English or a modified Arabic.

An Antonov bomber flies overhead on a weekly basis, circling, looking for victims, all civilians on this sacred piece of earth. Sometimes the plane drops one bomb, sometimes eight, sometimes more than twenty. Sometimes no bombs are dropped; the plane hovers over the area, terrorizing the people, then flies off and returns five minutes later. The clinic was bombed in September 2000. For the next two years, until it was rebuilt, over one hundred patients a day were taken care of in the open air, under the trees.

Of course, there have been casualties because there are not enough bunkers. Recently, with the help of a Sudanese laborer who helped us hand-manufacture cement blocks, we built a ten-foot by four-foot underground bunker with an eight-inch thick reinforced concrete top. It is meant for about fifteen people, but more can be squeezed in.

We had one of the worst bombing experiences toward the end of 2000. On that day there were many children from the nearby school around the compound. When the bomber suddenly appeared, we filled the two bunkers near to us, but there wasn't enough space; many of us sprawled stomach down on the dirt and covered our heads. I was lying next to Sister Madeline and put my arm around her. A young girl, about eight years old, crawled between us. I could feel her heart pounding.

Other youngsters were all around us, and some were crying. We prayed a litany, which helped all of us stay calm. The bomber circled, coming lower and lower. It dropped twelve bombs just a short distance from where we were cowering.

One of the bombs did not explode. I took a picture of it sticking out of the earth, broken and sharp, desecrating the ground. On the one side is our compound, an oasis, a vision of a future, and on the other the unexploded bomb. It is like the two sides of humanity, the one positive and reinforcing, the other deadly and self-destructive.

After a bombing, there is deep silence. Not even the birds are heard, and it feels, sometimes, as though our hearts have stopped beating. Tears roll down the children's faces as they emerge from the bunker. We have nothing to offer them but our love and warm embrace, a presence that says, "We care!" Together with them, and their parents, and everyone who lives here, I am learning not to allow the fear of the bombing control me. I pray especially that the Sudanese people's suffering and their willingness to forgive the perpetrators of this war will eventually break the cycle of violence.

At night, rats scurry over the tin roofs and gnaw into our floor and walls. Like the war, they are insatiable. Although we have three bedrooms in our modest house, only one is rat-proof. I sleep there with Sister Madeline.

We are grateful for our dwelling and for the labor that has

Sr. Theresa Baldini greeting friends. (Maryknoll/Sean Sprague)

made our House of Prayer and Peace available for others to imbibe prayer and peace in their lives. We have no ceiling, though we are planning to construct one soon; it will make the rooms a bit cooler and also prevent the insect world from dropping on us. We do have mosquito nets, which make us feel more secure at night. The net catches scorpions, centipedes, and other insects, but we cannot be protected from the mosquitoes all the time. I, too, have had malaria more times than I can count.

And the rats. We have to live with those, too. Our cat, Angel, named after my mother, Angelina, stalks these long-tailed creatures, though we have never seen her catch one.

We set the clock for 5:30 a.m. Normally, we would arise earlier for prayer, but we need to wait past dawn until most of the rats retreat. How unrelenting they are, a model of determination. Nor do they mind the heat or suffer from debilitating fevers or complain. They teach us to meet all challenges, surviving, flourishing!

Any physical labor is done in the morning hours, when it is slightly cooler–90 degrees instead of the afternoon high of 100-120 degrees. Though I am no longer young, I try not to ask any worker to do anything I wouldn't do myself. This includes climbing up onto roofs and digging in the garden where we are trying to grow some vegetables. We have learned from the villagers to plant sukuma wiki–similar to spinach–and cow-pea leaves, both iron-rich green vegetables, as well as maize. The displaced population also receives rations distributed by Catholic Relief Services and/or the UN World Food Program. Sister Madeline and I live on lentils, peanut butter and crackers, cabbage (which can last about three weeks without refrigeration), and some fruit bought in the market town of Lokichoggio in Northern Kenya, a four-hour journey, though it is only about fifty kilometers away. This is because there are no paved roads in South Sudan;

roads are either very bad, extremely bad, or completely impassable. We travel north about once a month under a UN armed escort, and never at night. Bandits hide in the bush and attack convoys even in daylight hours. This means that we must stay in Lokichoggio overnight and return to Narus the following day.

The will to survive among the Sudanese is strong. They build their homes from scratch, they plant and harvest, they raise their children. An organization, the Sudanese Women's Voice for Peace, meets to discuss constructive ways to assist those traumatized by the war. There are many tribes in the village living peaceably, though many do not speak the same language. It reminds me of what could be–what must be–eventually.

Whenever people from outside Sudan come to visit Bishop Taban, he invites all the people in and around the compound to share a meal with his guests. Everyone contributes what little he or she has to the festivities. It is always a delightful gathering and has the feeling of family.

Life goes on, despite the war. Suffering is transformed, and we share a glimpse of love in simple moments. I do believe St. Paul's precept that when a person is weak, God is even more present.

Part Three

Fragile Peace

A young girl stands before a shrapnel-pocked wall on a rooftop above the Jenin refugee camp on the West Bank in May 2002, three weeks after a siege by Israeli Defense Forces. (David Snyder)

The stories in this section take place in countries or regions recovering from war where the culture of peace is no longer a distant dream; it is an imminent reality. Un-armed uniformed peacekeepers—the soldiers with the blue hats—have replaced peacemakers, or armed peace enforcers. All are donated by UN member-states; the UN has no standing army. Their work is dangerous; since 1948, 1,650 military and civilian peacekeepers have been killed. It is no wonder that there is reluctance on the part of UN member-states to donate their forces.

Whether the conflicts have been long or short, all have brutalized and uprooted the civilian population, mostly the elderly, women, and children. Eighty percent of afflicted war victims are women and children. During a conflict, the young men are either soldiers, or they are dead.

The announcement of a ceasefire and a negotiated peace settlement is a bonanza for the aid agencies as donations pour in. A "lead" agency is usually designated by the UN, and some coordination is attempted so that services are not duplicated. Repatriation of refugees and internally displaced people begins, families are reunited, the dead are buried in proper graves, landmines are marked for disposal, schools reopened, soldiers disarmed. It can be a skittish, difficult time, as evidence is gathered for international war-crimes tribunals, or new governments are elected, or factions begin fighting one another in the refugee camps or in distant villages. Alongside hope and a feeling of renewal, there may still be intimidation, assassination, continuing hunger, despair.

An area considered secure may become volatile, literally overnight. The peace may be so fragile, in fact, that it collapses, necessitating yet another evacuation of humanitarian workers. Or it may hold, enabling the disaster relief work to segue into development work.

Dr. Ellinas in Thailand. On his lap, a Khmer girl whose brother has just recovered.
(Courtesy Dr. Ellinas)

12 *Camp-bo-dia*
Thailand

Dr. Panayotis A. Ellinas

"I soon learned that nobody knows what to do with such treatment failures. Where does one go when guidelines dead-end? Even omnipotent western medicine cannot answer this question."

I was raw and idealistic when I arrived at the Khmer Rouge Refugee Camp on the Thai-Cambodian border in October 1998. I had just completed two medical specialties and a graduate degree in public health. I thought I had all it takes to be a good doctor.

I was born on a beautiful though tragic island, the island of Cyprus. As a child I witnessed napalm bombs, death, destruction, and occupation. A scene with pained faces comes back to me often: family and friends fleeing from the bombs and all the ones who didn't make it silenced in mass graves. This is what led me to my vocation.

I was hired by the American Refugee Committee (ARC) after a two-hour long-distance telephone interview; I was still in Atlanta when they called from Thailand. I tried to match what they said with the "Terms of Reference" for the job they had sent me, but I can't say I understood the description any better by the time I put down the phone: "To promote maximum individual and community involvement in the planning and operation of health care services."

My official title was clinical coordinator, and I was to replace Dr. Z, who was going on leave. The plan was to keep him at the camp until I arrived so that I could ask him questions and learn hands-on what I needed to know about the

post. But as soon as I got there, I had to begin to work immediately.

When I arrived, throngs of refugees in traditional Khmer
dress and headscarves, accompanied by scores of ever-pres-
ent dogs, besieged the top of the hill. I jumped off the truck,
thankful for the unparalleled traction of my fancy Doc
Martens (which were to be, wisely, from that day on,
replaced by my sturdier Garmont hiking boots) and hurried
after Dr. Z. He had already made his way amid a parting sea
of people and disappeared under the straw roof of the clinic.
The Khmer paramedics awkwardly greeted him as they
attempted to grasp every fifth word he mumbled; our Thai
staff did not fare any better.

The clinic was an open-air structure with a long thatched
roof. Several dozen patients were lying on the ground on
bamboo mats. The floor was muddy and scores of dogs were
scavenging, lapping, and licking at human remains and
excrement, seeking shelter from sun, rain, and hunger alike.
An occasional IV bag hung from bamboos; a puddle of dry
blood from the night's last amputation discolored even the
angry bright-red clay dirt floor. Dr. Z asked the head medic
to "disinfect" that spot; soon a layer of fresh sand lay over the
dried-up blood pool.

I walked down the long passage between the bamboo
mats. I shivered, even though the weather was hot and
humid. Patients and their relatives scrutinized me with pierc-
ing eyes. What could they have been thinking about or hoping for?

Most of the patients were amputees. All were young
males, austere looking, once defiant, now broken and
maimed. Most had lost one limb—a foot, a leg below the knee,
a whole leg up to the hip—or, sometimes, both legs. The anti-
tank landmines were unforgiving to those who survived
them. I struggled to find a middle ground for my uneasy

gaze, lower than their burning eyes, higher than the vacant stare of their bloody stubs.

Apart from Dr. Z, who was leaving, there was only one other doctor in the camp, Dr. L, a graduate of medical school in Ho Chi Minh City. Her official title was reproductive health coordinator, but she was, of course, much more than that. She spoke Khmer, her native language, as well as Cantonese and Vietnamese. She could also get by in Thai and French. She was indispensable as a translator, and her medical skills were outstanding. All my book learning was no match for her. Nonetheless, because she was "local," her salary was much lower than mine. She had left her family and child in Cambodia to take the job.

All the paramedics were Khmer. They received token pay, even though their skills were often sophisticated. "They may seem a little rusty and hesitant when it comes to treating a simple fever or an upper respiratory tract infection," Dr. Z said, "but you should see how the spring into action when a landmine injury comes in. They do the whole amputation and control the bleeding in no time. Years of field experience! I just stand and watch."

"What kind of anesthesia and analgesics do they use?" I asked.

"I've written a memo requesting an exception to policy because of the unusual circumstances here; nothing yet, we have no anesthesia, no pain killers, nothing, just some paracetamol . . ."

What policy? There was a great deal I didn't understand.

The refugee community in the camp was thought to be about fifteen thousand, a slippery figure that sometimes grew to more than thirty thousand in an "official" count. But even if it was just fifteen thousand, that was a daunting physician-to-patient ratio. This was not a normal population, after all. The refugees had suffered war, displacement, disease, amputation, and many other traumas. And they had been involved, as perpetrators or victims, in genocide.

It is not widely known that this particular piece of Thailand has never really been under Thai control. It long served as a Khmer Rouge stronghold and operational base. It is thus no wonder that the Royal Thai Marines had such a reluctant presence there. This being one of the most heavily mined and malaria-infested regions in the world, coupled with the sheer apprehension and fear the words Khmer Rouge continued to elicit, were plenty for these Thai Marines to think about at night as they huddled under their pesticide-impregnated mosquito nets, sweaty fingers glued to the trigger. They knew as well as anyone that their best weaponry was no match for the hardy Khmer Rouge.

Many camp occupants continued to fight with the Khmer Rouge in Cambodia and returned to the camp for R&R, so to speak, and/or much needed medical care for their wounds and endless bouts with malaria. Many others went back to plant or harvest their land and crops, care for their livestock and properties, sometimes just a stone's throw away on the other side of the Cardamon Mountains. Or they'd simply head for the jungle to search for traditional diet edibles to supplement their World Food Program (WFP)–procured diet. In the jungle or the fields they would often encounter landmines. Landmine injuries, malaria, and malnutrition were the biggest medical problems in the camp.

A small, hilly promontory immediately on the other side of the river had been stripped of all vegetation, of anything alive, really, to make room for the clinic. I thought this a perfect metaphor for the suffering in the camp. There it was, a dead, bleeding, decomposing landscape. The mutilated clearing already had visible signs of advanced erosion; human folly had cleared the way for the relentless monsoon downpours. Wafts of silky mist and smoky morning fires pranced

A Khmer refugee camp in Thailand, run with the aid of the International Red Cross. (UN Photo 152259/Sam Levin)

about in the subtle morning breeze, dancing like dandelion blossoms to the howling rhythm of dog serenades.

On my third day I was called to see a patient who had been brought in during the night. He was still dressed in Khmer Rouge combat fatigues, and his injuries were serious enough to have merited being brought straight to the clinic for referral to the local provincial hospital for surgery. My supervisor had a fit when he saw me treating this man.

"This is not a military hospital," he said.

I treated him anyway.

Just days later, Dr. Z was gone. On my first morning alone at the clinic, three children with malarial parasitaemia were waiting for me. They had been admitted overnight. The medics chuckled as they told me they were all repeat customers.

I soon learned that nobody knows what to do with such treatment failures. Where does one go when guidelines dead-end? Even omnipotent western medicine cannot answer this question.

It was time to come face to face with what I had inherited from Dr. Z. He had made a point of remaining detached, and his English was so poor that I could not ask him questions and get a coherent answer, even if I had known what questions to ask. In the precious little time we overlapped, I learned practically nothing regarding the scope of my daily duties as clinical coordinator. The stained patient charts were lying hidden under bamboo mats, protected from gusts of rain and wind and the voracious wild dogs that tried to eat everything in sight. I didn't know where to begin and felt overwhelmed.

And then Dr. L appeared. She looked at me with kindness and seemed to understand my predicament. She started chatting, asking, poking, and chuckling with the patients in Khmer. She was connecting, helping, consoling. We went on our rounds, together with the paramedics. Antibiotic courses were stopped, changed, or became the foci for teaching discussions. The patients watched quietly as we gathered round and perused their charts.

The forays around the camp to make house calls were a challenge. The wheels of our monster 4-wheelers spun in the gravel and mud, dogs blocked our path, and waves of children followed us, eager to catch a glimpse of the farlang, the foreigner. Like children everywhere, they were just curious, never loud or disrespectful. Often they quietly gave front-row space to a playmate on crutches, and this touched me.

There was a thriving black market on the fringes of the camp. Stolen Thai cars, motorcycles, and anything else for which there was a demand were promptly supplied. Even aid-distributed mosquito netting and medicine were for sale there. I assumed it was stolen but didn't ask too many questions. There was talk that drivers employed by the aid agencies were involved in drug smuggling. During my tour in the camp, amphetamines were the hottest drug on the market. They were very popular with Bangkok yuppies.

One afternoon another landmine victim, this time from within the camp in an area that was supposedly "de-mined" and "safe," was brought into the clinic. He was gently lowered on a mat that covered a bamboo bed. We still had no narcotics or anesthetics, and we never would, despite repeated requests, during the many months I worked at the camp.

"How about diazepam?" I said.

"Oh, they've already given it," Dr. L said.

"Yes, 10 mg doctor," whispered Nyn, the head medic, in his soft, soothing voice.

I jumped on the truck to go with the patient to the provincial hospital. My assistant, Jacques, was taken aback. He later told me that no expatriate doctor had ever offered to go to the hospital with a victim before.

The next day I headed for the Thai Marine base across the shallow stream; rainy season had long been over. I was going over to ask for a bomb squad to accompany me to the #2 section, where this latest incident had occurred. Everyone knew that this section was littered with unexploded ordnance and landmines. The Thai Marines certainly knew, too, but did not feel obliged to do anything about it, nor had they been ordered to do so. Months earlier, unopposed Hun Sen thugs first heavily shelled and then invaded the camp, assassinating several much sought-after camp members, some in the sanctum of the clinic and in front of the Royal Thai Marines' eyes. I wasn't there that day—it was before I arrived at the camp— but I heard about it, and I knew if there was trouble we could not count on any protection or help from them. I thought I'd try anyway and wasn't surprised when they refused.

Then, one day, as I was examining a patient with a damaged heart and thinking about the high-tech surgery available in the West, I heard explosions in the background. The Khmers matter-of-factly mumbled, "It's still far." But it wasn't. I wondered if the Thai Marines would rally their forces, even though I knew that expectation was hopeless.

Our staff's response was almost instantaneous, however, as machine-gun crackle gave way to the annoying hiss of walkie-talkies. Suddenly, I was being shoved toward a truck, its engine already revving. Against my will I was being evacuated and dragged away from my patients.

We crossed the river at a rapid clip to where the Thai Marines were waiting for us. This was our "safe haven," we were told, though we knew otherwise. Gathered together in that spot, we were, in fact, a much more strategic target than if we had been left in the camp. The Thai Marines were scared, and there weren't enough of them. They could easily be disposed of with a few well-aimed big-gun shells, and us with them.

Our motorcade was lined up in characteristic military orderliness in anticipation of a hurried flight deeper into Thai territory when two calm figures in flip-flops approached us, our chief medics, Nyn and Heing. They spoke softly to Dr. L through the lowered truck window, Jacques listening intently in the back.

After they finished talking, they stepped aside and I waited for Dr. L to translate.

"A landmine victim just came in," she said.

"Please, doctor," Jacques said.

He had been in an evacuation before my arrival and left the injured behind. He did not want to repeat this.

There was no question in my mind, none at all: we had to go back.

That night Jacques and I drank a few brews on the roof of the clinic. My head fell back as I let my tired eyes roam the horizon and blend with the evening sky. I felt limp.

I thought of the evacuation protocol and its purpose—to protect the humanitarian workers—and the conflict this raised in me as a physician. I wanted to have a choice: to go or to stay. Meetings with supervisors were always frustrating and rarely touched on these personal and ethical issues. Our laundry bills were too high, and they wanted us to be more frugal.

DECEMBER 11, 1998, was the coldest day I ever experienced in Thailand. I needed to warm up and headed to the shower. I soon realized, however, that the water temperature in the shower did not vary at all with ambient temperature, as it should, but remained a constant "extremely cold" or at best, "refreshing," depending on the exuberance of one's morning mood. Even the mosquitoes remained snuggled up somewhere and didn't dare come out to find their morning meal: me.

When I arrived at the clinic, Pen, the medic on duty, was wearing a tee-shirt with a standard NGO team-spirit-inducing motto blazoned across his chest. He was shivering and his hands trembled when he tried to bring them together to respectfully bid me good morning.

"Very cold today!" I said from inside my Patagonia designer thermal undershirt, mock-turtle neck, Milanese safari-vest that Alessandro and Marina had given me, and my bright red, beautiful, Gore-Tex North Face jacket.

It was ridiculous. Offering to share a few of my layers at this point would be humiliating to this noble soul.

Huay Cherng Camp for Cambodian refugees in Thailand. (UNHCR/K. Singhaseni)

"You don't have a jacket at home, Pen, something with long sleeves?"

I gestured with my hands at my multiple layers of long sleeves for added clarity.

"No," he replied, not in a way that begged to be pitied but in a matter-of-fact way suggesting that of course he would be wearing it if he had one.

I walked away and sat down. I had already decided that I was going to send a jacket for Pen the following morning. But I still felt horrible.

SOMETIMES THE CAMP was inexplicably quiet. There were no shells exploding, no howling dogs, no crying babies. During these mysterious and welcome respites, we'd unconsciously rest a bit, slip into neutral, and talk more informally.

One day, during such a lull in activity, I was explaining the origin and function of the NGO that had paid us a visit that day. The Khmers' curiosity had peaked as the men in drab official clothes with starched collars had climbed out of a 4-wheeler that bore Cambodian license plates. These men were members of CMAC–the Cambodian Mine Action Centre–and had come from Battambang. They had been invited by the UN High Commissioner for Refugees (UNHCR) to assess the feasibility of both carving a mine-free route back for the refugees and de-mining Samlot–the area where UNHCR planned to repatriate the refugees.

"Two-to-three hectares per month per brigade–which is a group of twenty-nine men," their head person had said. "And that's if we can pull all our men away from all other regions."

They showed us a color-filled map of Cambodia. It resembled a topographical map from afar, but once one got closer the terrifying truth blasted us right in the face. Red, yellow, purple, and blue shadings did not signify altitude, arable land, or mountain ranges. The thousands of blue dots represented landmines, red indicated American B52 bombing targets, and so on. The number of unexploded American bombs and Chinese, Khmer, and Vietnamese landmines was staggering. Some are surface deep; some are many feet in the ground, depending on how heavy they are and from what altitude they were dropped.

De-mining would take years, but as reconciliation talks between the political leaders continued, it was obvious that repatriation wouldn't wait. The refugees were eager for it, also. Rumors abounded in the camp. The first was that Thailand was reclaiming its land and kicking the refugees out, relieved, at long last, to be rid of them. The second was that the land in Samlot was going fast, and they had to get there quickly.

The UNHCR, mindful of the agricultural cycle and the need to plant before another rainy season, encouraged the idea of repatriation. But I was concerned and alarmed. All the homes in Samlot had been dismantled and the materials long sold to the emergent and thriving construction industry in Battambang, the second largest city in Cambodia. And I could not stop thinking about the map of unexploded ordnance.

When I asked my medics why the people were leaving at such an inopportune time, it was not long before I realized–with Dr. L's invaluable help, of course–that many simply did not know they did not have to leave, that under international law repatriation must be voluntary. Either this was not explained well to them, or they did not understand.

So an exodus began, and then the defeated return of refugees coming back to the camp for treatment. After a period of declining death rate, we were suddenly faced with significant increases in adult typhoid cases and diarrhea. The water in the camp was potable, but the water in Samlot was not; the refugees were bringing typhoid back with them. Cerebral malaria, landmine injuries, and, tragically, even cholera completed the grim picture.

It was the cholera that caught the attention of the newly appointed UNHCR representative in Thailand. He urged me to put what I told him in writing and fax it to him at his office. He was due to leave for Cambodia for further deliberations with Cambodian and Thai officials regarding the repatriation package our refugees were to receive, and he said that he wanted to take my letter with him to the meeting.

I followed up with yet another letter addressed to the UNHCR in which Dr. L and I proposed an interim cross-border health clinic until medical services could be established in Samlot. This could not be done, we were told, but

A Cambodian refugee awaits transfer to her final destination. (UNHCR/K. Singhaseni)

our paramedics were repatriated to Samlot with a very unofficial and very large load of medical supplies, thanks to a supervisor with a big heart.

One of the cholera victims was the daughter of General

Ien Phan, a sometimes camp resident and one of General—"the Butcher"—Ta Mok's henchmen. Ta Mok was the only remaining Khmer Rouge leader not to have agreed on a truce with the Hun Sen government. He had been arrested and while in custody was making deals with everyone.

General Ta Muth, another of Ta Mok's henchmen, was also in the camp. In fact, he was our camp's military leader and by coincidence was General Ta Mok's son-in-law. All these men, I continued to remind myself, were deeply implicated in the genocide.

So here I was, ministering to the daughter of a butcher's henchman.

Dr. L had met General Ien Phan and found him "reasonable." I didn't know if she was being facetious or not, and I suppose it didn't matter in the circumstances. There was no question of not treating his daughter.

The UNHCR representative came to see us to discuss medical screening for repatriation. The Médecins Sans Frontières (MSF) book has a section on this, all of which is common sense. The seriously ill, peri-operative, and peri-partum were all to delay their departure until they were fit to travel. Then there were what the UNHCR calls "special cases" that require special handling: the amputees, the blind, the mentally disabled, the orphans, the single-female households, and so on.

The registration took place at the UNHCR shack. Some of our previously downsized staff members were hired back as interviewers. The families then proceeded to the clinic, where health cards were examined and children's immunizations updated. Then the families posed for a picture with the head of household holding a giant identification number in front of them. The backdrop was a blue rain tarp with the UNHCR insignia clumsily taped on it.

The refugees were scared. They had already been through so much. What would await them in Samlot?

Dr. L chatted with each family in her usual relaxed and forgiving style. She brought out the best in everyone, including me, and never lost an opportunity to counsel or educate.

I leaned back and let the back of my head rest against the post, seated on the bamboo bench half-smiling at the sight of Dr. L, tirelessly performing her unending array of miracles. Golden arrows from the setting sun were now skimming the impenetrable jungle gloom, ricocheting off the bright-green canopy as it disappeared in the thick, humid jungle air.

A well-dressed woman handed her papers to Thia, a medic. Another single parent household, I thought. Her two children were equally well groomed and well behaved; she knew today was picture day. She asked Thia why other amputees were getting something scribbled on their papers but not her. She had gone through the interview and screening without having her disability noticed; no one noticed that she was an amputee, one of a handful of female landmine victims in the camp. Her husband had subsequently left her.

Then a man stood before us wearing dark glasses. Three children quietly stood around him, the eldest acting as his seeing guide. The man suffered from chronic pulmonary infections; the landmine that had gutted both his eyes had also ravaged his chest wall and many pieces were still inside. That same landmine killed the children's mother.

I was deep in contemplative mode when I sensed that a man was talking to me. He was very ill and would be allowed to stay in the camp.

"Thank you very much for helping me," he said.

I didn't know what to say, so I just nodded my head and pressed his hand gently. It was an unending procession of sorrows. We did the best we could and screened carefully.

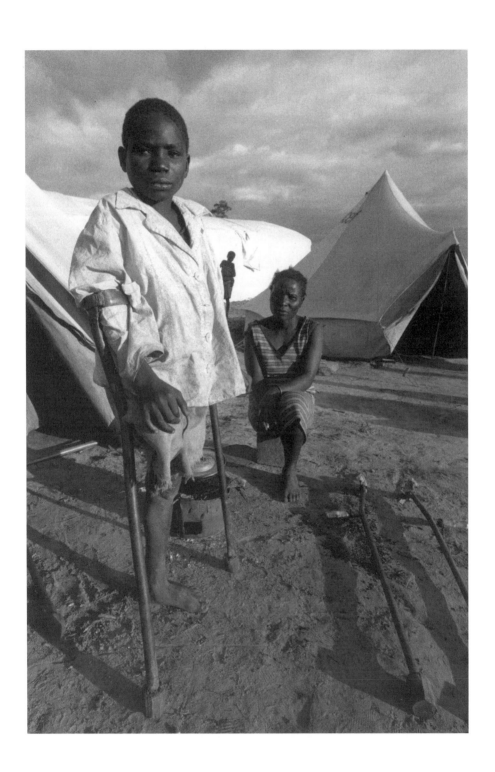

13 *Letters Home*
Angola

Paul Heslop

"We should have a break every three months no matter how much we enjoy walking into a minefield every day and dealing with thousands of UXOs. It definitely starts to play on the back of your mind."

**The Halo Trust
Kuito, Angola**

1995

7 March

I had a great leave, and now I'm back. Let me tell you about my adventures since leaving Heathrow. We stopped at Zaire and most of the people got off, so while we were on the ground I walked up to first class and stole all the magazines and newspapers including the French ones to give to the Médecins Sans Frontières (MSF) doctors back in Kuito. I knew that would earn me some brownie points with them. The plane was nearly empty after Zaire so I had four seats to myself and got a couple of hours kip. Tuesday we got a message asking us to call Kuito urgently so we were all shitting ourselves thinking there had been an accident. Fortunately Ski hadn't blown himself up, but he had malaria, so I had to get

Domingos, 12, who lost a leg to a landmine, stands in front of tents where he now lives at Campo Minars, a UNICEF-assisted center for people displaced by the war. His mother, Marguarida, who also lost a leg to a landmine explosion, sits behind him, her crutches on the ground. (UNICEF/HQ96-0086/Giacomo Pirozzi)

into Kuito as quickly as possible. The flight the next morning was meant to be at 6 a.m. Our car is broken at the moment so I had to go up to the airport on the motorbike with the computer over one shoulder, the camera over the other, the cold bag between my legs on the fuel tank, and a sixty-pound rucksack on my back. What a nightmare! Still, where there is a will there is a way. When I got to the airport the pilots weren't there so I had to wait for an hour for them to show, and then they announced the flight to Kuito wasn't until noon.

8 March

Had a visit today from the British Embassy, so I'm going to give this letter to them and get it posted in the UK. Between running one team, trying to recruit a second to start training the week after next, surveying the town, doing unexploded ordnance (UXO) clearance, and visits by every Tom, Dick, and Harry, I'm running round like a headless chicken. The peace process seems to be breaking down at the moment, so hostilities may start again. We are quite a long way back from the front line–approximately twenty miles–so nothing much to worry about, but a German expat was ambushed last week about 250 miles away and killed, so we are all being mega careful.

17 March

Hopefully, this letter will have a Dutch stamp on it as I am sending it along with someone leaving this place.

I destroyed over sixty UXOs this month and have found loads more. We had a bloody reporter here for three days who was a pain in the arse; she was doing a documentary on the UN in Angola by the BBC. They want to film de-mining and are coming back next Thursday for three days, so I might be a star. They want me to blow a few things up, so I've found a mortar stuck in the road in the middle of town and a dump of fifty more that will make a hell of a big bang. The program

Paul Heslop in Angola.
(Courtesy Paul Heslop)

is going to be called "Under a Blue Flag," all about the UN in Angola, and is going out in October.

Things are fairly quiet here in terms of the war, but there was a little bit of shelling last Saturday about twenty kilometres away. I have found a great new house for us to move into; it has lots of parking and high walls all around, five bedrooms and plenty of storage space. Have got quite a good crew of expats in Kuito at the moment so we have a good laugh most Saturday nights when we get together at one of the houses and have a few beers. I do my party trick of falling asleep on the sofa as all the rest go to the disco.

Kuito seems to be getting rebuilt slowly by the people living here, and the town looks so much better than in November. It's still got that shot-up look, but more houses have roofs now and quite a few of the schools have reopened. I've been back nearly three weeks, but it seems more like three months. Well, I'll say bye for now.

23 March

Life has been hectic as usual. John Findley finally got back from South Africa on Friday so at least there are two of us here now. Last week there were three accidents and this week two. That's about treble what it has been for the last couple of months. We are trying to find out why the sudden spurt and if somebody is putting down new mines. So far this month we have destroyed over 120 items. I'm trying to think if I have any remotely funny stories to tell, but none springs to mind at the moment.

28 March

Let me fill you in on why the last couple of days were so hectic. The BBC was still here yesterday morning and wanted to interview me before flying out at 9:30. We also had a new training course starting and instead of the expected forty new recruits, sixty-two turned up, so this all added to the confusion. Then there was a big bang about a mile away. I thought, Shit, that's down near MSF. So John and I charged back to the house to get the protective gear and the big first-aid kit, and we were just about to set off when a message comes over the radio that the accident was near the market and it was a Concern vehicle. We managed to fight our way through the crowds and saw the crater; it was about two meters wide and a meter deep. My first thought was: Where is the bloody car? It had been blown completely over, and about twenty feet off the track. To say it was mangled would be the biggest understatement I have ever made. I went over to the cab very carefully, expecting to see blood and mutilation, but the cab was empty. The first locals on the scene had got the three guys out of the cab. I couldn't believe any of them could be alive.

John and I started an investigation into the type of mine that had exploded. I was surprised that with all the people at the nearby market there weren't shrapnel injuries, but everyone was OK.

We had been at the site about five minutes when we heard a bloke screaming. I went over to investigate and found a one-legged man with a long cut in his arm. He was worried he would lose his arm, too, so we loaded him in the back of the Land Rover and I took off to the hospital at top speed with the horn blasting. I plowed straight through a funeral, which probably has put me on some family's death list.

Today has been a bit less frantic but still kept us busy. This afternoon we blew up sixty mortars, which made a very satisfying bang and a very big hole. I still can't believe I get paid to blow things up nearly every day. Well, best get on with cooking some dinner or it will be beans and rice again.

7 April

I'm still bunged up with cold. I just don't seem to be able to get rid of it. I don't know if I mentioned it before but we have a new doctor here, a thirty-eight-year-old Scot with a good sense of humour, so I am trying to shock her senseless at the moment. She has already commented on the fact that the other expats' language and behaviour deteriorates in my presence. My response was that I've always been a bad influence on everyone I meet. But she is getting bored at the moment because the MSF hospital is so good here—it even has a surgeon—so we don't really need a doctor, she's redundant. We are trying to find her an interpreter so she can help out at the MSF hospital as a casualty doctor, but interpreters are short on the ground in Kuito, so she may be leaving us soon. This seems a shame as she has given up three months of her time to come out and help.

9 April

We are helping the police clear all the unexploded stuff they have down at the bombed-out police station. But he keeps trying to tell us what to move and when. Except we are the supposed experts, it is our vehicles we are using, and it's our bits that get blown off if there is an accident. He wanted us to move and destroy about a hundred rockets that were hanging around. But the fuses on them are very sensitive to temperature changes, which can induce a current into the fuse and trigger the explosives. We stood in the middle of a room full of unexploded bombs and rockets while the police chief waved this rocket around telling us it was completely safe. Finally, we left him to it and told him we would be back on an overcast day when there wouldn't be a temperature difference between outside and inside the store. I don't think there'll be much of a police station left by the time we are done as most of it will have to be blown up.

The afternoon was very good. We had been invited by some Italians building a hospital to go round for a BBQ. It started at three and by nine I was so stuffed I could hardly move. I had an early night last night and got a good ten hours' kip, which I feel great for. Today looks like it will be a

A mine removal specialist with the British NGO Halo Trust probes for landmines in a field outside the town of Kuito, Angola. (UNICEF/HQ96-0091/Giacomo Pirozzi)

lazy day with just a few bits of paper work to catch up on. We have been invited to Concern for dinner, which I think is going to be a roast. We will pop there around five and help cook. I'm going to teach them how to make Yorkshire puds after my success with Christmas lunch back in December.

11 April

We had a delegation of American congressmen and the ambassador today. What a waste of time. They arrived late, had a meeting with all the charities for about ten minutes, drove round town, and left. The situation in respect to mine accidents to locals is getting worse at the moment. Loads of women are having accidents digging new fields or collecting wood. I saw a poor little boy of eleven who lost his leg on Friday. I didn't realise how much fat is between the skin and the flesh on a leg. I was in the operating theatre today as they were amputating a woman's leg. It was very interesting until they got the saw out. Then I had to leave. What a wimp, eh?

12 April

It's been quite a busy day for me. Firstly charging round trying to get letters posted by people going out. Then back to the house to see how it's coming on. Most of the house now has a roof! So it looks like we might manage to get moved in next weekend with a bit of luck.

Then I went down to hospital to see if I could get any information about either the woman who stood on a mine yesterday or about the soldier who stood on one last week. The woman was still half doped from the operation yesterday so I will try and speak to her tomorrow, but they said the soldier was just about to be operated on and hadn't yet been anaesthetised and did I want to speak to him, so I said sure thing. My god, what a smell. It was unbelievable. The poor bastard stood on a mine five days ago and has been in the military hospital ever since. He had his foot completely blown off and part of his hand as well. He was quite lucid and told us exactly where he was when he had the accident and what he was doing. I found myself watching the second amputation in two days. I didn't realise I had the stomach for it. Christ, when they took his dressings off all the flesh from his lower leg had been blown off and partially cauterised, it was black, and all the rest was green and had maggots in it. There is no way I could be a surgeon or nurse and see that every day. It took hours for the taste of the smell to get out of the back of my throat.

Then, on the way home, at the side of the road, I found six rockets and four mortars so I cleared them to stop someone else having an accident. I spent the rest of the afternoon at a little old man's house where I cleared four mortars from his garden. John found over a hundred mortars in Cunge, which is about five miles away, so it looks like there will be a big bang on Saturday.

13 April

Went up to Cunge to investigate the accident involving the soldier who blew his foot and hand off. Got up to the military area where it happened and had a chat with the local commander. The poor guy had gone to pick some avocados and stood on a mine under the tree.

Back in Kuito I popped round to the hospital to see the woman who stood on a mine on Monday to find out where it was only to find out the poor woman had been six months pregnant at the time and was undergoing a miscarriage as I arrived.

22 April

God, I love my job. I just got back from a town called Chitembo about 150 kilometres south of here, a tar road all the way although very potholed to start with. It is deep inside

UNITA (Union for the Total Independence of Angola) territory. It was very interesting to see what it is like on their side of the front line. Things change once you go through the UNITA checkpoint; the road is in immaculate condition and the countryside and villages look more like Mozambique. People seem relatively well fed, but they don't even use money, everything is bartered, with salt and soap being the benchmark for prices. Compared to Kuito, there is almost no war damage; most of the roofs are on and the buildings are not full of bullet holes.

Chitembo is meant to have a population of fifty thousand, but we didn't see anywhere near that number of people. Everyone was really friendly. They were really happy to see us, especially the UNICEF guy who had soap, blankets, and medicine to distribute. We had the usual meeting with all the head guys of the village and I even managed for most of it without an interpreter. After about eighteen months, I can now just about grasp a bit of Portuguese.

They don't seem to have a big mine problem in Chitembo. There are nowhere near as many amputees proportionately around the town as there are in Kuito. But that doesn't mean I had no work to do. They took me to a South African booby trap which I disarmed and blew up this morning along with a big rocket we found on the side of the road, so I was popular with the locals. But I was completely knackered yesterday so I passed out about 8 p.m. last night and didn't wake up until 7.30 a.m. Nearly twelve hours of glorious kip! We have a new guy coming on Monday and Rodney in two weeks so hopefully the work load will reduce a bit. By the end of the month, I think we will break the thousand mark for explosive items cleared and destroyed this year, so we must be doing some good.

Got a fax from home which was great. I've had no post at all for over three weeks and I was starting to get a bit depressed. I feel like I am completely out of touch.

25 April

Well, the biggest bit of news is we have moved into the new house. The roof is OK, the paint has dried, the generator is connected properly, and the toilet even drains. I'm chuffed to bits. Well, a girl is going back to UK tomorrow and will be there until the 17th of May. If you want to send any letters to her, she will bring them back with her straight to Kuito, so no problems with the Angolan post. I have not received anything this month apart from the fax last week.

The second training course for locals is finished so I now have ninety-five de-miners plus support staff and I need to recruit at least another seventy. It's getting to be a big operation here.

28 May

Seven weeks tomorrow I leave Kuito to start the trip home, thank god. I love what I'm doing but at the moment I've had enough. I feel like I've been here three years not three months. This week has been fairly busy as always. Rodney arrived Monday afternoon, Tuesday was spent showing him round, Wednesday a delegation from Swedish Relief arrived. They are rebuilding the road between here and Huambo. Thursday I drove to Huambo with them to assess the need to de-mine the bridge heads that have been blown. One thing for certain, somebody in UNITA knew exactly what he was doing. Every bridge between here and Huambo had been dropped perfectly so they have to be totally rebuilt, none can be repaired. Fortunately, it looks like only one will need to be de-mined. The road, however, is totally mined. It was like being back in Mozambique; it took ten hours to drive 105 miles.

Huambo is a lovely city hardly damaged by the war. It would have been gorgeous in 1975. Unfortunately, however, just before we got there, one of the buildings used by Concern collapsed. Many injured, they had all been rushed to hospital and treated by the time I arrived so no need to pull the rubber gloves on, thank god. We drove back on Friday and as we didn't have to keep stopping to look at bridges, it took less time. The countryside is beautiful but there is no wildlife, not even birds; all have been shot and eaten during the war. I wonder if in fifty years there will be any game left in Africa.

Tomorrow I am heading back into Luanda, then I've got to fly down to the Namibian border to deal with a load of rockets, mortars, and shells CARE dug up while doing a water project, so that will hopefully make a big bang. I'm going to try and stop off at Lobito on the way back and say hello to the Brits. I got a fax from T. the other night. She is going to be in Luanda on Tuesday, so I'm going to try and meet up with her, which will be excellent if it comes off.

12 June

This morning, a guy came round saying he had a mine in his garden. Rodney and I popped round to investigate. There was a trip wire that started in the garden and went off to the side. The wire led to a skeleton. This was the guy who had tripped the mine, so there was no need to de-mine that one. All in a day's work in Kuito.

20 June

Hi, back again. I don't know where time has gone over the last three weeks. I just seem to have been running round in circles. I know I haven't written since I went down to Lubango, which is a city to the south of Angola about five or six hours drive from Namibia. The CARE folks dug up a load of tank rounds and asked for someone to go and sort them out so I volunteered myself.

Lubango is like another country: the town is intact, the shops have things for sale, there is a sort of calm. On the cliffs overlooking the town is a huge statue of Christ, like the one in Rio. I spent the night there and headed down to Cahama on Friday only to be seriously pissed off. A German charity who does similar things to us had beaten me to it and removed five tons of ordnance. It looked like I had just travelled on one long enormous goose chase. I was asked to do the final sweep in case anything had been missed. So off we went. We arrived at a bunker complex where there were two still-armed surface-to-air missile launchers, eight missiles in all. The launchers were wrecked, but the missiles were still intact. Talk about excited, I nearly peed myself.

Everyone was worried that I would launch the missiles if I tried to defuse them. Finally, I got the administrator to agree to let me take the missiles off the launchers and blow them in a nearby bunker. The problem was getting them off. I had no idea where to start. One of them was loose, so we unclipped that one and lowered it gently to the ground. The rest proved a bit harder but after fiddling around for a few minutes I found a catch. It was stiff, wouldn't come loose, so I resorted to the big hammer approach: I gave it a good kick. That worked except that everyone watching nearly had kittens. To be truthful, my heart was in my mouth. Got them to the bunker but due to a shortage of explosives, I was only able to knock the warheads off. I'll have to go back another day to take care of the propellant.

6 July

Leave is getting very close now. I get off the plane in London two weeks from today and to say I'm looking forward to it would be an understatement. Things are busy here. It's just Rodney and me at the moment so we have lots to get on with. Have had quite a good week really. Went down to Chitembo again last Saturday to destroy the eighty rockets I found there last time. Then on the way back, there was nobody at the UNITA checkpoint so I hit the horn a few

Beneficiaries of Halo's work. This village has been cleared of mines. (Halo Trust)

times, still nobody turns up, so John says, "I'll get out and lower the barrier." As we were driving away, I looked in my mirror to see this guy waving and gesturing in a none too friendly manner, then bang bang bang, he started shooting at us. I floored the gas pedal and kept going.

I got five letters last week, a miracle. I've sent 254 letters and received forty-one, not the most impressive ratio.

11 July

Hello again. Well, only a week to go now. Have just done a mine/UXO assessment for the World Food Program (WFP) and popped into their office. A new base manager, Helen, was there and we started talking. She came round for a mine awareness brief and left scared shitless. She arrived here, one of the most dangerous places in Angola, possibly in the world, with no accident, health, life, job, or injury insurance.

Found yet another skeleton yesterday. You can't go anywhere without coming across some grisly reminder of the war. People are too scared to go out and even bury their dead.

30 August

Yesterday morning, while fiddling with one of the Land Rovers, there was an explosion about 300 meters away so Terry and I grabbed the first-aid kit and stretcher and charged off. A large crowd was gathered around a little girl laid half in and half out of a river. She'd obviously triggered a mine and was unconscious. Everyone was too scared to go and get her in case there were other mines. In we went, with a couple of locals, to get her on the stretcher, but by the time we got her to the hospital, she was dead. I've seen some horrible things since I came here, but this was definitely the worst. Bits of her skull were sticking out.

Yet another film crew here as well, so I'll be a movie star yet. Gave them a good show. There are loads of rockets that have failed to explode around town but are about a meter long and stuck in the ground with only about 20 centimeters of the tail showing, so I have come up with a technique of chopping the tail off with a few twists of detonation cord, then filling a condom with TNT and dropping it down the rocket so it is behind the warhead. It works a treat.

24 September

With Rodney gone and Steve on a remote task I'm here by myself most of the time and running four teams at once. We got permission to clear one of the defensive minefields last week and took out just under a hundred mines in eight days. Good experience for the guys I trained here. Also one of my de-miners showed me a 250 kg air-dropped bomb the other day which should make a fucking good bang when I blow it. My only worry: it is in the main river running through town and if it is white phosphorus or nerve agent it could kill half the town when I blow it.

Did anybody see the article in *The Economist* of 16 September on Kuito? The journalist who wrote it came here a couple of weeks ago with a delegation from the US. She was absolutely petrified after my safety brief and almost cried with relief when she got back on the plane.

Have been invited round to MSF tonight. They have killed a pig, so I made a marinade and we are going to have a meat feast tonight.

16 November

Well, first the bad news. Tits, a local I trained to de-mine, went tits up on Sunday and was buried with full Halo honours half an hour later. The Brazilian contingent has now arrived and is setting up camp on a site I cleared a couple of weeks ago. The two new Land Rovers arrived in Lobito today but the Angolan customs are being particularly unhelpful, as usual, so we probably won't see them before Christmas by which time all the kit in the back will have been stolen, which includes the personal stuff I bought when I was last on leave.

On to happier things: no mine accidents this week, no parties planned either, so all very quiet on the social front. We have changed our working hours because it is starting to get bloody hot in the middle of the day.

21 November

I'm suffering from an extremely bad stomach upset at the moment and feeling sorry for myself so I thought I'd write a quick note. I got a letter from Tom and one from Mum the other day via Switzerland and a copy of *The Economist*. I haven't read any really good books for ages so keep your eyes open for me. I was looking at MBAs again in *The Economist.* It would be nice to come back to the UK for a year to study again.

22 November

Still suffering from an upset stomach so I will go onto Flagil tomorrow if no improvement, which means no beer for a week as it induces nausea and sickness if mixed with alcohol. The BBC is coming out at the end of this week again so maybe I will get to appear on the news or something else equally exciting. I am sick of journalists. The other piece of news is one of my de-miners stood on a mine yesterday. He is one of the luckiest bastards alive–he only set the detonator off so there was a pop rather than a bang and he was completely unhurt. He was breaking the safety rules walking in an uncleared area. I'm bloody glad he still has his leg.

21 December

On Thursday there was a mine accident on the Chipeta road. A CARE truck drove over an anti-tank mine. So Terry and I piled in the car with all the necessary kit and charged off again. We passed a CARE car and then a WFP car coming the other way. We flagged it down and they said it was "only" an anti-personnel mine. To which I said, "That is even worse; somebody is going to lose a leg trying to change the tyre."

The accident turns out to be on the same stretch of road as the big accident in April, on the bit the governor had said was safe because the army had de-mined it. We knew it wasn't and had marked off a safe detour which everyone was meant to use. The CARE truck driver, for some reason, ignored the detour. So when the CARE base manager arrived, I gave him a bollocking for not contacting us and for not making his staff take the detour.

1996

5 January

Just had a few minutes to spare before yet another governor's meeting so I thought I would put fingers to keyboard. Usually these meetings go on and on, mostly complaints by the Angolans about the NGOs doing nothing and taking responsibility themselves for making all the difference here.

The first week of the new year is over without too much excitement, although yesterday I got a fright when I heard Giles on the radio report a mine accident, two killed, and thought it was some of the de-miners. I turned out to be an accident about 5 kilometres outside of town–a woman and a twelve-year-old boy triggered a jumping mine. By the time I arrived they were carrying the bodies out of the bush to much wailing and gnashing of teeth. I called for a pickup to take the bodies back to the family.

Woke up on Wednesday feeling really shit so didn't drink any alcohol all day (first time in months). Still felt crap yesterday so I went for another malaria test, but it was negative.

Getting on well with Giles, who is turning out to be a real asset. He just gets on with the jobs he is given, no problems, but he is a sleep monster in the morning. He also likes to cook so the two of us take turns each night. Last night I baked a steak and mushroom pie which turned out well so I was chuffed to bits. We then had a game of Risk with the American girl from AFRICARE. It's the second time this week I have trashed her and what a bad loser she is. It must be the American attitude that they are unbeatable until they get their arses kicked, and then they sulk. Tomorrow we are going to clean up all the explosive junk outside the house and blow it to snot and back which should be a satisfying bang.

18 January

Well, it's funny how some days you absolutely love your

job and some days you don't. Yesterday, I woke up about 4 a.m. feeling really dodgy. Giles kept bringing me cups of sweet black tea. He's a good bloke.

Tomorrow we have two delegations, French and American. I'll take them to the minefield, then scare them shitless with my safety brief, and then plug for the money. It usually works and most of them are so scared they never come back.

So yet another new face, a nurse. There is also a new logistician and anaesthetist arriving tomorrow. I wonder how many people have been through Kuito since I arrived. Just Rona, Dale, and I seem to be the constant; nobody else has any staying power. Well, I fly out three weeks tomorrow, and I am definitely ready for it. We should have a break every three months no matter how much we enjoy walking into a minefield every day and dealing with thousands of UXOs. It definitely starts to play on the back of your mind. To be honest, I've had a few really weird dreams lately where I am stuck in the middle of a minefield with loads and loads of really tricky booby traps to deal with before I get out. Keep well and I will see you soon.

23 January

I've had a hectic time since I last wrote. The two delegations have come and gone. There was an armed soldier every ten meters from the airport to the minefield and back via the hospital, an armored car at every junction, and there must of been at least fifty UN cars at the airport to transport everybody. The plane was met by an honor guard who played the Brazilian national anthem as the ambassador got off the plane. Fortunately, I spotted Chris Simpson from the BBC world service—he lives in the HALO house in Luanda—and walked over to him in the middle of the national anthem. "How's life, you fat bastard?" I asked. He was very embarrassed.

The convoy set out for the minefield. Chaos ruled. It doesn't help that the field is a dead-end so there were cars trying to turn round everywhere. I eventually managed to get order and stood on the bonnet of my Land Rover and screamed: "Good afternoon everybody. My name is Paul and the safety brief I'm about to give you could save your fucking life, so stop pissing about and listen in."

This got their attention so I managed to give a pretty good safety brief although I doubt CNN could transmit it due to the number of bleeps in it. I then took them into the mine-field and answered all the questions as we went. We had rigged up a charge about 150 meters away and we got Madeline Albright to press the button, so she blew up a mine to great applause. All the time CNN was taping. She turned to me and asked me how I got involved in de-mining, to which I answered completely deadpan, "I rang them up and asked for a job." Everybody burst into hysterics. If you saw me on CNN, let me know if it was a good performance.

1997

27 January

Another year, still here in Angola. I love the job but am really looking forward to leaving. Christmas dinner went off very well. I managed to get all the food on the table at around the same time so it was all hot. And the Yorkshire pudding was perfect. I didn't burn it this year. I wonder if I will have a fourth Christmas in Kuito. Three so far.

I guess you know about the Princess Di visit by now. She was going to visit on Wednesday so I planned to move to Huambo on Tuesday to make sure everything was OK. I was going to leave early on the Tuesday morning but for some reason felt very uneasy about that, so I thought I would just wait until lunchtime before going. I must be psychic because at 10 o'clock I get a call from the ICRC saying I was needed at the airport. She was on her way to make a surprise visit; the itinerary had been changed. I then pointed out I'm meant to be in Huambo to take her through the minefield there, so I managed to persuade them to let me get on the plane when she left Kuito and fly down with them to Huambo.

First a plane with journalists arrived so I gave them a safety brief. Then Princess Di arrived. She is an extremely beautiful woman. I gave her a safety brief but she didn't seem to listen and was very evasive with her eyes and body language, so I was worried that she wasn't paying attention. Finally, we left the airport, with twenty-three police cars charging around with sirens flashing, and lots of men with guns everywhere.

After the tour of the Kuito minefield, I boarded the plane for Huambo. I was meant to be in a seat at the back of the plane and got on last, but my seat was taken and the only seat available was directly opposite the princess, so I sat in it and started to chat. I remembered I had a bag of mints in my pocket so got it out and offered it round. They were accepted by all; the ice was broken. The conversation wandered over a few things but when we got onto mine accidents, I think a couple of people felt a bit queasy.

The flight was only twenty-five minutes so we were quickly back on the ground. While Di went off to meet the governor of Huambo, I headed for the minefield. The guys had done a great job and it was all extremely well marked out and very clear with press box, briefing area, etc. We waited about forty minutes for Princess Di to arrive and I then introduced her to the rest of the crew. I did a safety brief again and put her into the safety gear, with a big HALO patch sewn on. Free advertising, we figured.

Then, onto the minefield. Princess Di did really well in the minefield. She was a lot less nervous than some HALO expats on their first visit into a mined area, or the delegations we've been escorting from all over the world. We walked up and down a few times. I showed her the mine she was going to blow up, as the photographers kept snapping.

14 Out of Time
Afghanistan

John Sifton

"Down the road some civilians have been buried in the ground—the refugees who were blown up while trying to flee. War here has caused its inevitable and common consequence: collateral effects on civilian life."

When Afghanistan was under the Taliban, life was tense but time was slow.

When I first landed in Kabul, in the spring of 2001, I remember feeling as though I had just stepped back in time, or out of it, and was in a historical play about simpler but more brutal times. On the runway in Kabul, Taliban soldiers had stood languidly with their long black robes, beards, and rifles. They stared at us as we got off the plane and averted their eyes when some women doctors from an aid organization appeared. I remember how, as soon as the plane landed, some of the women on the plane—old hands in Afghanistan— had lifted their chadors over their heads and adjusted their clothes. We had walked over the tarmac, across the broken asphalt, into the dark, quiet Kabul airport. We sat in the damp visa office on weird furniture as a sad-looking Talib official thumbed through our passports. He looked up now and then to compare our faces with the pictures, narrowing his eyes and then making notes in his ledger. We had spoken softly, if at all, and we dared not laugh. A clock lightly ticked in the corner. I had felt like a child in a strict school.

And now it is March 2002, a year later, and all of that is gone. I am flying on a UN plane from Islamabad to Kandahar

John Sifton in Afghanistan. (Courtesy John Sifton)

into an Afghanistan sans Taliban. I have already been to Kabul, teeming with its thousands of journalists and new aid workers, and to sleepy old Herat. I am working for a human rights group, gathering information about the conduct of some of the local warlords, new allies of the US-led coalition in Afghanistan, who have taken control of most of the country's territory. I am also arranging logistics—cars, housing, interpreters—and conducting some preliminary research for a comprehensive survey on the bombing in Afghanistan, including an estimation of the number of civilian casualties during the air war. I am already totally exhausted, though I have only been in the country for two weeks, so I doze for most of the trip, missing the spectacular mountains on the way.

I awake as we are descending into Kandahar airport, bouncing in the air turbulence, the plane rattling us about like dice in a cup. As we bank for landing, I look out the window. The Kandahar airport has become a US military camp: tents, troop carriers, jeeps. There is a large military transport plane sitting on the tarmac and combat helicopters along the runway. Sandbag bunkers pepper the base, little bumpy squares, long high-caliber weapons protruding from within. It is impressive, given the history of the place. The best the Taliban ever mustered here were a few old Russian tanks, mortars, an ancient set of transport planes, some Toyota trucks. Now, by contrast, the Americans have built a fortress of canvas, sandbags, and tedious military professionalism.

Bomb craters and destroyed military equipment still line the airport's periphery, a common sight on all Afghan airfields. Before the United States ever came to Afghanistan, the airports in Kabul and Mazar were littered with old combat garbage and the tangled wings and tails of airplanes. It is difficult to separate out which parts of the destruction are new and which are the product of decades-long conflict. Old Soviet MiG fighters blown into halves mingle with Taliban transport trucks hit mere months ago—steel from different wars twisted together in the sand.

Our little plane lands on the broad runway, no problems in the gusty wind but, strangely, we taxi right past the main terminal, an odd high-modernist 1960s structure half destroyed by neglect and war. We continue on past the control tower on the top of which flies an American flag, the only American flag I have seen except at the American Embassy in Kabul. We turn around and taxi back down the runway, past the tents, a city of military offices and dwellings; past the military hardware and more compounds, including a small gym with weights and large, shirtless, tan men lifting them (again, odd). We come to a stop at the very end of the airport where a small UN bus is waiting next to an army vehicle and two American officers in fatigues, soft canvas hats, mirrored sunglasses, and mustaches.

"Welcome to Kandahar!" one of them chirps as we deplane.

"Same to you," someone mutters.

No one responds directly to the officer's welcome. Most of us on the plane are humanitarian aid workers, diplomats, or human rights advocates, some new to Afghanistan, others not, but we are not inclined to be cheery with these military officers, no matter their nationality or how gregarious they are. It reflects a humanitarian elitism of some sort; most aid workers are from a different world than military folk. We have different aesthetics, ethics, and educations. It's just the way it is. The pilots do strike up a conversation with the officers eventually, but most of us walk past them to get our bags, glum and aloof.

We then stand for some moments on the tarmac, blinking in the bright sun, waiting for supplies to be loaded from the bus into the plane. In the distance, pairs of US Army troops are jogging toward us: exercise for the garrisoned troops. A football is being tossed back and forth. A jeep rumbles past. The driver calls to one of the officers near us, laughing: "Hey Pete, what's going on? You giving these people a hard time?"

"How are you, man?" Pete responds. "You learn how to drive yet?"

Jokers. We could be on a base in North Carolina.

One of the officers happens to pass by me. "How are you today, sir?" The chipper voice is dissonant. "I'm fine," I say.

I look over at a fellow passenger, a European diplomatic officer whom I talked to on the plane. Like me, he is a human rights specialist, and I know that he has been to some of the "dark places of the earth." I know this because he has told me, but also because I have seen the way he pauses before saying certain things; it is an effort just to maintain the consciousness to speak, an effort to reconcile his experiences of hell on earth with the act of keeping up a cheerful conversation with a complete stranger.

The diplomat is tall, thin, and very pale. He stands in his wool sports jacket, beads of sweat popping out of his head, reflecting the sunlight. His eyes have grown wide as though he is in a trance. This look is familiar to me, and I think I can read his mind. All of this, he is thinking, these strange sights and sounds, these glib Americans, this trash humor, it is so absolutely out of place and somehow wrong. There are refugee camps mere miles from here, with their disease, graves, scabs, terrifying testimony from survivors of atrocities. There are villages in the hills where people have sold their children as servants to buy food. It is somehow wrong that these men do not appreciate the proximity of the horror or have blocked it out and are basically, well, fucking around. Obviously, back in Brussels and New York, people are having their dogs shampooed and are ordering the Nacho special–humanitarian workers have to consider the horror of such juxtapositions all the time–but these people are right here in Afghanistan. This mundane Pax Americana at Kandahar airport is apparently more than the diplomat can stand. I can see it all in his eyes. He almost looks like he wants to vomit. I want to vomit.

Meanwhile, the American officer is still joking, asking me if I have brought them any hot dogs or soda. I look at him and smile, make the joke apology: No, I haven't brought anything.

I want to ask the officer why there is an American flag flying on the top of the control tower. This is not American territory, and there is no such flag at the Kabul airport. I want to tell the officer how much it pisses off Afghans to see something like that, but I figure they must consider this an American base, and that is the policy: Fly the American flag. I remember something about the American flag from the World Trade Center being flown here in Kandahar, a ragged pennant someone found in the rubble in New York. An image to boost morale.

I was there, in New York, when the towers fell. Just home from Kabul, I had rushed downtown and stood in the dust and smoke at City Hall with a whole crew of ad hoc rescue volunteers. I had seen the fires, the dazed firemen, and I had felt the shock of Afghanistan in New York, the shock I had felt in seeing the dead and starving, Talibs beating women, the effects of the war. I felt as though one country's insanity had been brought to another. Then I saw the United States slip into an unabashed full-on patriotism that made me feel uneasy and disgusted. I had seen the image of Olympic athletes, in corporation-branded patriotic clothing, carrying the American flag, a silly merging of logos—Reebok, Fidelity Investments, stars and stripes—beamed around the world. And I had felt like an alien.

And now I live to see Kandahar again. I see the US Army soldiers jogging past in Nike shorts (aliens here, but not alienated), with the American flag in the distance, hoisted over Afghan soil, images of patriotism and commercialism. A complete and meaningless circle.

I happen to glance over at the Beechcraft again. The other officer is leaning up against it, chatting with the co-pilot. The Beechcraft. Jesus. The UN plane is made by the Raytheon Corporation, an American company that makes Sidewinder missiles and the Tomahawks fired by US submarines. I want to laugh, albeit in a nasty, cynical way. What a circle, what a world! Standing there, I feel that it all is absurd and childish—flags, countries, corporations, military affairs, human rights workers—all of it seems to be contained within a big seamless stupid game: this base, our little plane, the UN, the naive soldiers in their sports gear, Afghanistan, world politics, people trying to get their little selfish tasks done.

So I know I am back in Afghanistan. Not because of the confused and vague sense of banality and despair, but because I am having a moment. This may be why I love this place: It lays things bare and makes the present seem so small. I seethe on, daydreaming as we wait for our bus to be loaded.

Finally, the truck starts up, breaking my reverie, and we climb aboard and drive out of the base and into the city of Kandahar.

"LIBERATED" KANDAHAR is bustling with business. Trucks laden with tires, plastic jugs, wood, food, are lined up on the road entering the city from the west. Police, troops, and truck drivers stand around, smoking and drinking tea. We speed through a maze of bicycles, taxis, and buses as we enter the city, our driver almost crashing into a donkey cart at the main city gate. Right on the main road, I see my local contacts—some staff at an Afghan aid group—and I tell the UN driver to stop. He pulls over, and we transfer my bags into their car. I say goodbye to my co-passengers and head off to the compound in which I will stay.

The city generally is intact. The bazaar, the old city, the so-called Red Mosque (now blue) are all standing, and there are few signs of the US air war. Most of the destruction is outside the city, in the military compounds and houses used by Taliban and Arab Al Qaeda leaders. We pass one "Arab house" in the west of the city, a cheesy 1970s knockoff stucco job, half of it blown away by bombs. Some children are playing on its remaining upper floor, running back and forth in some improvised game with a broken umbrella and a tangled Slinky.

"This was the house of my uncle," one of my Afghan hosts says. "The Taliban put the Arabs to live here. My uncle was put to another place, but they gave him some land."

A sort of eminent domain. I wonder if the uncle is pissed off at the Americans for destroying his house just as the Taliban were being crushed.

"Is your uncle angry with the Americans for blowing up his house?" I ask.

"What can he do? Some Arabs were there, with their families."

"The families were there when it was hit?"

"Oh, yes. Many families of the Arabs died here. Many Arab women and children. They are buried over in the east of the city. The Afghans left the city during the bombardment, but not the Arabs. Let me tell you: There is a grave place of Arabs in the east of the city, I will tell you about it. We say the Taliban and Al Qaeda are gone, but if that is true, then why do these people, from the city, they go out to this grave place and pray in the afternoons. These people still are here, these people of the Taliban. These people go out there and they roll on the ground, and act crazy, and speak words that don't mean anything."

"You mean like a religion thing?"

"No, no, this is not Islam, people acting like that, crazy. They are just stupid."

"We should go and visit," I say.

"Yes, maybe. Some time we will go."

There is one other major bombing site: in the very middle of the city lie the shattered remains of the Taliban's Ministry for the Promotion of Virtue and Suppression of Vice, formerly known by most aid workers as Vice and Virtue or, simply, V & V. The building, once a rather nice street-side brick building, has been flattened by a pair of American JDAMs (Joint Direct Attack Munitions)—two precision-guided bombs dropped from on high. Bricks are lying halfway into the street. A house across the street has also been hit, likely by accident. I am told that two civilians were killed.

Now, however, next to the old V & V some vendors are selling "Kandahar salad," a skinny head of light green lettuce with some dressing sprinkled over it. Men are lounging

Lina, 18, helps neighborhood children study in her home in Kabul. She completed the third grade before, like other girls under the Taliban regime, she was forced to stop school. Nevertheless, with the help of her brother, she continued her studies, and now helps others. (UNICEF/HQ01-0558/Shehzad Noorani)

around, music is playing, and some children are running by with their newly distributed UNICEF school bags. All this gaiety would surely never have been permitted by Vice and Virtue under the old regime, but now things are more relaxed. Yet I note with a sad shrug that all the women are still avec burqa.

I have to find a car or a truck. I also need an interpreter. At my new lodgings at a local aid organization, I tell my host—the head of the organization—about my needs. After some lunch he sends me off with Zaveed, an Afghan aid worker, to find the required services.

We climb into a Toyota station wagon to begin our search. "First we will go to car shops," Zaveed says as we are driving out of the compound. Car dealerships, a logical starting point.

I am hopeful that we can find what we need. Despite all the poverty in Afghanistan and Pakistan, there are bazaars in which it is possible to buy anything. "You could probably buy a nuclear submarine in Karachi," an American exile once joked with me in Peshawar. Supply and demand, on a crude scale. There is an infamous quote, by the pretentious nineteenth-century historian George Bancroft, etched into the wall of a certain bank in New York: "Commerce defies every wind, outrides every tempest, invades every zone." It is true, I suppose. I saw new televisions for sale in the streets of Prizren, Kosovo, six days after the Serb withdrawal in 1999. ("The fucked-up thing you can see here is that the revolution will be televised," said one aid worker to me.) So I am confident we will find a car: The laws of commerce ensure it.

Zaveed and I drive up to a car lot near the Red Mosque. "Fancy Cars" is written on the wall amid some other Pashto script. A man in a long brown sharwaz kamis and black turban greets us in English, inviting us into his small shack for tea. Declining the offer, Zaveed and I ask if any of the cars on the lot can be rented. The man considers. A long conversation then ensues, in Pashto, which I cannot understand. After a while, Zaveed turns to me.

"These trucks here can be rented for two hundred dollars for the day."

"No, no, no," I say. "That's absurd."

"This man says that they are new trucks."

"I can't pay that. In Kabul I paid someone twenty dollars a day. Tell them that I am not a journalist."

"I have said this to him. He will not bargain. Maybe 150 though."

"I could rent ten trucks at once in Kabul for the same price," I say. "Tell him."

"He is saying that he is of great need of money."

"But he is a car dealer. He is one of the richest people in Afghanistan."

"Yes, but he knows you have the money," Zaveed says matter of factly.

"All right, let's go."

As we walk back to the car, another man, who has been listening the whole time, says something more to Zaveed in Pashto, laughing.

"What did he say?" I ask as we get to the car.

"He said that you should buy a mare and ride around on her."

I GO WITH ZAVEED to a food-distribution site in the north of Kandahar, where Zaveed's organization is handing out fifty-kilogram bags of wheat to the residents of the city. We are still looking for a car to rent, and an interpreter, but we have stopped to observe how the food handout is going. "Maybe someone here will know about a car," adds Zaveed.

We stand inside the broad distribution compound, about ten acres inside a low wall, with twenty or so of Zaveed's colleagues and a handful of the city's residents. Four trucks are parked nearby, piled with bags of food. Outside, hundreds of Afghan men, women, and children stand around waiting for their turn to collect a bag. Many of the women, clad in their mini-pleated blue burqas, are crouching in the dust; as usual, they seem to be trying to make themselves as small as possible. In "ideal" cultural circumstances, these women would never leave their homes, let alone wait in line in public for food handouts, but as I have learned over the last year, nothing in Afghanistan is ideal—even the misogyny—so here they are.

Some soldiers—recruited recently by the United States to

fight the Taliban—stand at the gate, inspecting distribution tickets. They let in five or six people at a time. The admitted Afghans quickly walk up to the truck and gather bags of food. Some aid workers help the old women and children drag their bags back outside. A French aid worker stands at the gate, gathering the tickets of the people on their way out. At the gate, some people start yelling at the guards, pushing, and the guards start using sticks to beat back some children who have managed to sneak past the checkpoint.

Zaveed shakes his head. "The UN wants us to distribute this food to the people of the city. And now we have registered 350,000 people to get this food. But I do not know if there are 350,000 people in all Kandahar." He spits some tobacco juice into the sand. "I see the same people twice, and some people don't get anything at all. These soldiers are also asking for food."

"The soldiers?" I ask.

"Yes, it is true, They come to us and they say: 'Why don't you give something to us? We were fighting the Taliban. We should be given something also.' Or they bring someone else . . ."

"A brother, like?"

"Yes, like that, a brother, and they say: 'This man here did not receive a ticket. Please give him some food.' And we have to send them away. And still, at the end of the day twenty or thirty bags of wheat are not in the registration books; they have disappeared. And then the French lady from World Food Program comes up and asks us questions like a policeman. She is not very nice. She does not trust us. But we say, it is not us taking the wheat. It is the police people."

"The army troops, you mean?"

"Yes, the troops. But, believe me, these people are not troops. They are some people who the governor gave some guns."

"Like a month ago they were drinking tea in Pakistan," I say.

"Yes," Zaveed says, laughing. "They were drinking tea."

"Well, I agree with you," I say. "The French lady doesn't seem very nice."

"No, she is not very nice," says Zaveed. "She is very strict." And then he laughs again, "Like the Taliban."

We look over the gate, and I see a boy pressed up to the gate, about eight years old wearing big funny glasses with a big plastic nose and a fake mustache. He yells to me in Pashto: "I am an American!"

WE FINALLY FIND a truck in the west of the city, near the compound of the International Committee of the Red Cross. We have heard about it from a friend of Zaveed's, and when we get there, it all checks out. The truck is old but seemingly reliable, and cheap. The driver is a rather round and kind-looking man named Fassad. I arrange to rent his services for a week, and we drink a glass of tea together.

We soon also find an interpreter, at a private English school that Zaveed knows: a kind old gentleman named Ahmed who lived in the United States for almost twelve years and was deported after serving seven years in prison on a drug charge, a history totally incongruent with his appearance. After arranging our contract, Ahmed brings me into his classroom and introduces me to all of his students. I sit at the head of the class for about fifteen minutes as some of them ask questions. "Why are you here?" is the first and hardest to answer.

Finally, we head out to the car. Ahmed suggests that we go for a tour of the city and then have some dinner. We head off to the bazaar and the old city, where we have kebab, nan, and tea. As we drive through the narrow streets, people keep staring at me through the windows. I am used to this. I am a sight.

*An Afghan boy at Gudham Shahar Camp in Mazar-i-Sharif, Afghanistan,
December 2001. (UN/DPI Photo by Luke Powell)*

IT IS MORNING a few days later. I have made some introduc-
tions with the local government and met with local minority
groups to talk about their situation under the new authorities
and their hopes for the new government. Everyone seems to
love the leader of Afghanistan, Chairman Hamid Karzai, but
most are worried about local commanders, who they say are
"all warlords." There is a lot of fear about future instability:
warlords fighting with one another over territory.

Now I have to check out some of the bombing sites outside
the city, places where civilians may have died, to get a better
idea of where my organization's survey team needs to go.

I drive down to a small village south of Kandahar called Mullah Abdullah Kariz with some Afghan de-mining experts. I have made contact with the de-miners because they generally know best where the bombs have fallen; they are the ones who have to find (and defuse) the ones that don't go off. They want to show me Mullah Abdullah Kariz because they say it was struck extensively during the air campaign, predominately with cluster bombs—the infamous munition with its individually released "bomblets," which sometimes do not explode but instead land as duds, remaining in the soil, dangerous, like landmines.

We are on the highway south of Kandahar, a good (and rare) asphalt road, passing donkey carts, slower trucks, and old men on the side of the road offering their prayers to us for money. We are driving too fast for my comfort, but every mile or so we approach a crater from the US bombing and the driver slams down on the brakes; we slow almost to a stop and crawl slowly over the torn part of the road before racing on.

"Here, right here, is a place where a truck was hit by American bombs," says one of the Afghan de-miners at one point. "There is a grave, there, where the driver is buried." He points.

"A Taliban truck?" I ask. I am not interested so much in Taliban casualties.

"No, a truck, for business."

"So the Americans thought it was a Taliban truck, or some Arabs," I ask.

The truth is that I am only really interested in cases in which civilian deaths may have been violations of the laws of war, violations of the Geneva Conventions or customary laws of war. And, according to these provisions, when a military force believes that a specific target is in fact the enemy—a military target—then there is usually no violation of the laws of war, even if civilians are in fact killed by the strike. As long as the military force takes precautions to eliminate or minimize civilian deaths; as long as civilians are not deliberately or recklessly targeted; as long as the strike is not "indiscriminate" (for example, reckless or needlessly broad); and as long as the strike's "military objectives" are "proportionate" to whatever damage to civilians does occur, civilians can be legally killed in war. This is why I ask about what the Americans might have thought in bombing the truck.

"Yes, they must have thought what you say," my Afghan guide says. "The Taliban is seen moving many things to the airport through this road. But also people from this village over there were leaving those places."

He points to a village that is coming up on the right and continues. "They were on this road. People were killed in another place. I will show you the graves. A family of people, not Taliban. There are the graves."

He indicates three mounds on a small hill, about twenty-five feet from the road, with white flags posted above.

"Not Arabs?"

I had heard that a lot of Arabs—presumably Taliban fighters, possibly Al Qaeda—had been seen fleeing on the road toward Pakistan.

"No, not Arabs. The Afghan people. A man and two children."

We cut off the road, hitting a straight dirt road running next to an irrigation ditch. Though no longer on asphalt, the driver maintains the same speed. Rocks kick up into the wheel bases, noisily pinging the underside of the car. A massive cloud of dust is raised behind us.

"Here the Americans have bombed in many places," says the Afghan.

We are driving through agricultural land.

"But there is nothing here," I say.

"The Taliban was here. They moved their trucks in this

place. But when the Americans dropped the bombs the Taliban was not here anymore."

That's war, I think to myself. Battlefield intelligence goes stale faster than store-bought dinner rolls. What a waste, throwing all of that fire into the dirt, hitting nothing, scaring the hell out of children for miles in every direction.

"They did hit a few houses in the village beyond there, and some people were killed there, some families."

"Can we go there?"

"No. The place is near the airport, and the Americans will not allow you to go."

We pull off the dirt road onto a smaller dirt road cutting though some vineyards with rows and rows of grapevines leaning up against short mud walls built to support them.

"Here is the village," says my Afghan guide.

We drive through the vineyards, up to a compound, then around it, and then into a sort of alley between two mud agricultural buildings. "For grapes," says the driver. The farmers hang the grapes in the buildings to dry them, for raisins.

We get out of the car. Some children approach. I am nervous, waiting to be told where to stand. I don't want to prance onto a cluster bomb. My guide leads me over to the side of one of the buildings, next to a pomegranate orchard. He points to a hole in the side of the building and says "CBU," meaning a cluster bomblet. He explains, gesturing to the hole, that the bomblet has blown its front fuse (meant to pierce through tank armor) and torn a little hole into the mud-clay building. Suddenly, a man walks up from the other building and starts speaking hastily to my guide. Later I learn that he is the owner of the land–a farmer–eager to have the UN remove the remaining bombs from his orchards and vineyards.

My guide turns to me and says, "This man will come with us. We will show you the clusters."

He jumps over a ditch into the orchard, turns around, and

beckons us to follow. "Be careful. There are many bombs here."

We follow. Since it is March, the trees stand without leaves or fruit, and we can see clearly through the branches. A few dried-out old pomegranates lie on the ground. We walk about twenty feet and my guide stops.

"Mister John, here are some bombs."

He points over to the left, and there, lying in the dried mud among some trees that have been splintered apart, are some small yellow canisters about the size of half a poster tube. They are dented and dirt-streaked, but I can see some numbers written in black on the side. They are American, for sure; I have been taught the markings. These are cluster UXOs, unexploded ordnance, remnants of war.

The farmer hangs back, looking sour.

"We will clear these clusters in two days," says my guide. "This man here has to use this land. There are many more over there."

Most of the fruit trees have been blown into splintered three-foot-high stumps. There are scars and markings from shrapnel in the soil and in other trees and little craters every fifteen feet or so, and occasionally, a large crater from a conventional bomb. Soon we come to an area that has been totally destroyed by the bombs—no trees, nothing, just overturned soil without life, pocked with craters, an epicenter of the strike. The area was part of the orchard; now it is nothing at all.

"So, tell me the truth," I say. "And ask the farmer. Was the Taliban here?"

"Mister John, the Taliban was over there." And he points toward the main road. "Two or three kilometers away. They were in a school. The farmer said this to us. And, why would the Taliban be here?"

That is, why would they be hanging out in the middle of a pomegranate orchard?

The farmer is looking at me, as though I am going to explain why the bombs fell in the middle of his orchards and vineyards. Perhaps he expects that I will give him some money as compensation. He doesn't really know who I am, after all. I could be some rich man from America, come to pay him back for the damage done to his livelihood. But I have nothing to offer except my bearing witness to his misfortune and offering a theory as to why it occurred.

I consider the possibilities. If the Americans thought there was something here, what was it? The Taliban may have been moving military trucks on the dirt road, four hundred feet away, toward the airport; perhaps the Americans were aiming at something then. But there are no destroyed vehicles or military equipment of any kind here.

I ask about bodies: "Was anyone killed here?" The guide and the farmer insist that no bodies were found and that no one was killed and the farmer says he returned soon after the bombing and there was nothing. I am not sure if the farmer really knows, since they could have been removed by other troops, but he is adamant about this point.

So either the Americans were aiming at something on the road (or something near it) and because of human or mechanical error, they missed; or else they meant to hit this orchard because they thought there was a military target here (which there probably wasn't). But then again, perhaps the American strike was successful and some Taliban were killed here and then dragged away by retreating troops. But why would so much firepower be used to kill a few Taliban? Or perhaps there were a lot of them. Perhaps. My mind goes round and round.

In the end I realize that it is all but impossible to find out the truth, standing there. Perhaps my colleagues can bring the matter up with the Pentagon later, if there is a reason to do so, but that is not likely. I am standing amid a lingering fog of war.

One thing, however, is clear: The orchard belongs to the

farmer—a civilian target—and it has been extensively damaged. Down the road some civilians have been buried in the
ground—the refugees who were blown up while trying to flee.
War here has caused its inevitable and common consequence: collateral effects on civilian life. People with no love
or pathology for war have nevertheless been dragged into its
horror. As far as actual effect goes, I can think of no qualita-
tive difference between what happened to civilians on
September 11, 2001, and what happened to these Afghan
civilians a few months after. Obviously, these civilian victims
of war suffered no less than the civilian victims of terrorism.
In fact, they may have suffered more: food-and-water shortages, night after night of bombing (ground shaking, children
screaming), and the general instability all around them. I look
once again at the farmer but then have to look away. I am a
little ashamed, once again, by my incapacity to say anything.

We drive on to another village, farther south. My Afghan
guide wants to show me two houses that were destroyed in
the bombing, both civilian homes. We spend a long time
looking for the right village, driving into several areas, unable
to find it. Finally, an elder from one village offers to show us
the way. The local villagers approach, and after we explain
that we are looking for the houses that were hit by the bombing, they lead us to a large area of rubble at the end of a long
street. A small crowd gathers as we look over the destruction.

The site was once a compound of four families. Of those
who stayed during the bombing, eight are said to have been
killed here; all four houses are completely demolished. There
is a vague story about how one of the deceased took a sister to
the hospital in Kandahar as the Taliban were retreating from
the city. When they returned in their old truck the compound
was hit, leading most of the family to think that the Americans
had mistaken the old truck for a Taliban vehicle, following it
back to the compound and then bombing the compound.

Plausible, perhaps, considering how poor intelligence seems to have been during the bombing. But what bad luck for the dead: to die at the very end of twenty-three years of war.

I take some pictures of the survivors.

Driving back to the city, I can see more trucks entering the gate and carts with freshly harvested vegetables and fruits. Some builders are mixing cement in front of a new building, constructing a new facade. There is an upbeat mood. The Taliban has gone, and for the first time in years, there seems to be the possibility for stability and growth. Of course, big problems remain: Local minorities face discrimination, even beatings; political inequalities suggest future conflict; and the subjugation of female life continues. Poverty, the secondary curse of Afghanistan, has just been put at the top of the list of the country's ills.

Still, there has been positive change, and I have to admit reluctantly that in large part it has been the Americans down at the base, with their banal humor and humorless armaments, who have served as a catalyst. As we drive on, I reflect on this: Perhaps the most insidious thing about war is that every once in a while it seems to justify itself, thereby justifying all of its useless and evil manifestations as well. A curse disguised as a silver lining.

15 *Appointed Rounds*
Occupied Territories

MacKay Wolff

"It was exactly the job that most boys would describe as ideal, the same mix of altruist and actor that makes the fireman look heroic."

In November 1988, the first Palestinian *intifada* began; soon after, the UN agency responsible for Palestinian refugees responded by establishing two teams of refugee affairs officers (RAOs), one each for the West Bank and Gaza. In their second year of operation I became a member of the team covering the West Bank and East Jerusalem.

UNRWA (the United Nations Relief and Works Agency for Palestine Refugees) headquarters were in Vienna in those days, having been displaced from Beirut by its civil war. I was given a day of briefings there on the administrative aspects of the job; only at the very end of the process, when I was nearly out the door to fly to Jerusalem, did they show me a series of film clips of what the work actually involved. The soundtrack alone—screams and shots and everything in between—was enough to give me second thoughts, and more than one drink on the plane.

The nominal mandate of the RAOs was to protect the camps run by UNRWA. This initially covered the refugees living in the camps, and the facilities—schools, health clinics, and offices—serving the refugees. To protect, as is usually the case with the United Nations, means to observe and to report. The presence of the UN, in other words, did not alter the general course of the occupation or of the *intifada*, but instead diminished, at the margins, the number of persons arbitrari-

A street scene in the occupied Gaza Strip. (UNRWA Photo by G. Nehmeh, 1988)

ly harassed or detained or injured as a result of the conflict. The observation reports we wrote at the end of every day were sent from Jerusalem to Vienna. There, they were collated with similar reports from Gaza, and the summary shared with the UN General Assembly, which is the deliberative body UNRWA serves.

There are twenty camps in the West Bank alone; their combined population is less than a third of the territory's total. The physical and sociological divisions between refugees and non-refugees, though, are negligible. In terms of the effects of the Israeli occupation, the differences are none. The international humanitarian presence in the Occupied Territories was in any case scant even before the *intifada*; once it began, only UNRWA and the International Committee of the Red Cross (ICRC) maintained a regular, complementary presence there.

And so inevitably–because the populations were homogeneous, and because no legitimate observer could differentiate between refugee and non-refugee–our responsibilities expanded beyond the camps alone to cover the entire population of the West Bank, East Jerusalem, and Gaza.

At any given time ten RAOs were employed by UNRWA to work in the West Bank and East Jerusalem, and an equal number to serve in Gaza. All were international staff, usually from North America or Western Europe; there were an equal number of women and men. All of us lived in private apartments in East Jerusalem or its suburbs and commuted to work through a fluctuating number of military roadblocks. Our work schedule was quite progressive for a UN agency: three and a half days on, followed by two and a half days off. In practice, the schedule was rigorous, though, since each day's working hours generally ran from 5 a.m. to 10 p.m. or later. Violent situations could change direction so quickly and so unpredictably that we always had to be alert. Fatigue, then, was always a safety issue.

The first of our days off was lost to sleep, enough to accommodate mentally what had come before. For the remainder, we often spent the days together. Since most of our working days were spent in a car, we traveled out of town only infrequently. Given the cars' markings, when we did take a trip it was rarely into Israel. Instead, we usually drove down to the UN Beach Club in Gaza to trade war stories with our colleagues there.

MacKay Wolff, back in New York, working at UN Headquarters. (Courtesy MacKay Wolff)

An RAO always worked with a Palestinian partner, a refugee affairs assistant. This partner served as guide and translator, as well as a second pair of eyes and ears. Together, the two of us formed a sort of super-detective team, which is to say that we kept ourselves constantly on the move, looking for signs of trouble. And when trouble was spotted, we would swoop in to confront it. It was exactly the job that most boys would describe as ideal, the same mix of altruist and actor that makes the fireman look heroic.

All the senses were employed in the search for danger. Sight revealed the black smoke of burning tires or the cascading arcs of thrown stones or Molotov cocktails. Hearing conveyed the presence of stones, too, as well as of Israeli guns firing; we had also to listen for rumors of trouble or announcements of the same. Taste and smell helped vouch for the accuracy of sight and sound, and for the presence of teargas.

With experience, we also developed a sense of "touch" for situations that threatened to turn more violent. This involved observing a crowd of Palestinians in a town or in a camp and learning to recognize, by its movements, when trouble was imminent. The way people moved in response to the appearance of an Israeli patrol, and how the patrol reacted to them, predicted a lot. The usual progression into violence was palpable, like a chemical reaction seen in a glass beaker. The Israelis regularly provoked this response, as a demonstration both of their freedom of movement through the Occupied Territories and of their need to control the ever-furious people living there.

This was especially poignant in the case of children walking to primary and secondary school. As a rule, the procession of half-awake children to their classrooms was uneventful. When an Israeli patrol of six to ten soldiers appeared, however, the results were predictable, and predictably intense. Stones would fly at the soldiers, who would in turn fire teargas and rubber bullets; arrests would be made and, frequently, the school closed for the day or longer. Other than as a chance to show off their superior power, since they were not serving any police function, the benefit to the State of Israel of these school-time patrols was not evident.

No matter how fierce the clashes between the Israelis and Palestinians became, I never felt any fear in intervening. This was so because I believed so deeply in the rightness of the UN's role in the conflict, at least as it played out on the ground. That sort of confidence was truly a prerequisite for doing the work; only by remaining calm and patient in violent situations could the observer observe, or intercede, with any credibility.

To be driven by passion was a stupid mistake under any and all circumstances. It reduced the effectiveness of the work and diminished the dignity of the organization; emotion made you look bad. The fact that we were not armed ourselves, and wore no more protection than fluorescent-orange traffic-policemen vests, conveyed another layer of self-assurance, much like that which journalists working in conflict feel by placing the word "PRESS" all over their cars and clothing.

That feeling of rightness also put the issues of bravery and heroism (or foolishness, for that matter) in perspective: it rendered them irrelevant, even inapplicable to the situation. Since what we were doing was right, rightness alone was the complete measure of our work. Ascribing finer qualities to the work, to the duty, would be gratuitous and plainly self-serving.

On the other hand, the refugee affairs assistants were far more vulnerable than we, their foreign partners. We, after all, were also protected by our nationalities–no small irony for UN employees–and would, at the end of our mandatory one-year tenure, leave for another posting. The Palestinians were there for the long term and so were compelled to exercise more caution in dealing with the Israelis, and show more deference to them, than we outsiders did.

Many of these political and cultural nuances could not help but emerge in the long conversations that took place as we drove on our appointed rounds. Most local staff in any UN or NGO field operation are drawn from the elite of the community–for all of the good and bad that that fact entails–and UNRWA was no exception. All of the assistants were university graduates. Their interpretations of history and current events were always interesting and often provocative. I was good friends with all of my partners and was optimistic for their success in other endeavors. Still, I feel certain that their sense of the evanescence of our work pushed them more toward hopelessness than mine did.

We drove unassuming company cars–Volkswagen Passat station wagons–since larger "utility" vehicles like Land Cruisers were thought to look too powerful, too military. This was unfortunate, since the punishment they were subjected to from both sides required something stronger. The cars were hit by stones and rubber bullets as a matter of course, but were also rammed by Israeli jeeps. Given the ruggedness of the terrain over which they passed, they also suffered from too-low clearance off the ground, and, running over the nails and broken glass that littered the streets, usually suffered at least two flat tires per day. The cars were painted white, with "UN" painted in large blue letters on the hood and the doors. They were equipped with VHF radios that allowed communication among teams and with the main UNRWA office in Jerusalem, as well as a very simple first aid kit. For the ostensible (if nonsensical) reason of impartiality, no kind of camera was allowed in the car during working hours.

Once a clash had begun, our task was fairly straightforward. My partner and I approached as closely as possible but did not enter into the line of fire between the two sides. We looked both ways, as if to cross a busy street, and then, depending upon the extent and duration of the violence, did one of three things:

I could speak directly with the Israeli soldier commanding the patrols or to the soldiers as a group asking them to ease up on the attack. These sorts of request were rarely successful, even as they were customarily posed when the attack was nearly over anyway. There was nothing the UN could do to stop an Israeli commander from embarking on an attack; it could only try to limit the damage that the hostilities caused.

My partner and I could pass behind the Palestinian lines to evacuate the wounded. This was a less useful, less efficient action, because the trip to a clinic or hospital took us away from our most important responsibility as observers. It was necessary at times, however, on the principle that we had to be seen to be doing something, especially in the most violent clashes. If a wounded Palestinian was taken by the Israelis, then he was unreachable; the fact of his being wounded was taken, illogically, as proof of his culpability. This equation was also applied to some Palestinians who were able to reach hospitals independently—the military would sweep through after the day's hostilities were over and take them from their beds directly to prison.

Most often, we would simply stand and witness the clash,

Gaza during the Palestinian uprising in Israeli-occupied territories during the first intifada *in 1988. (UNRWA Photo by G. Nehmeh, 1988)*

taking no action to stop it, even when the two sides could be seen, cartoon-like, approaching each other blindly and unaware. Once the fighting was over, visits were made to the regional hospitals to record the names and ages of the wounded and to the central military office to petition for the release of minors, those under the age of sixteen who might have been picked up. Even these interventions were for the most part pro forma, since the Israelis could and often did deny the UN entrance to military bases. They could also fine or arrest the parents in lieu of the child when the parents

ANOTHER DAY IN PARADISE

came themselves to seek the child's release. In certain cases the Israelis would demolish the family's home as a very public warning to the community of the dangers of protest.

As is true with so much of human rights observation, it is impossible to tell what might have happened in its absence. Success in protecting human rights was as variable as the characters of the people involved in the effort. After all, RAOs had no arms and no cameras–only the spoken word–to achieve their ends. Those words, and the human rights conventions to which Israel is a signatory, were the only pacific force in the conflict. And yet, ultimately, and as has been proven in the faltering of the Oslo accords, no external entity can substitute indefinitely for an indigenous, functioning political system.

The form of humanitarian action that the RAO represented was, in retrospect, unique in its immediacy. We made our case and knew within moments whether we had succeeded or not. This interval between action and result was the shortest I have ever seen, in the range that stretches through the delivery of supplies and advocacy for human rights to the confection of multi-year development plans.

For this reason, among others, it bears mention too that the form of coexistence that developed among the three sides–Israelis, Palestinians, and UN–during the first *intifada* would not be possible under the second one. In fact, it is inconceivable that any international humanitarian force could serve the same function again under the present circumstances. I believe this not only because both sides are more violent, but because the neutral space that the United Nations occupied–the space that supported its role as impartial observer and relief agency–has vanished.

MY TENURE in the West Bank as a human rights observer was in fact the second time I had worked there. In the early 1980s, I was the second of two internationals serving Catholic Relief

Services (CRS) there. The program was relatively rich, comprising rural development and mother-child health projects as well as a large supplementary-feeding scheme. I worked on all of these and also developed projects on my own initiative.

One of the better ones, I thought, was a proposed revolving loan fund for Palestinian families whose homes had been demolished by the Israelis as punishment for the misdeeds of a family member. Since these families were usually expelled from home in less time than it took to save their belongings, the idea was to loan them money for short-term needs–to pay rent on a new place, buy food and clothing, secure legal aid–until they were reestablished. This project was seen as politically inflammatory by CRS headquarters and, ultimately, by the Israelis; the humanitarian aspect of the idea was worthless compared to its political ramifications. Although I had intended to stay on with another agency after my first CRS contract was completed, I was instead denied a visa and a work permit and so was forbidden to return.

MY SECOND TOUR, with the UN, also ended unnaturally. With less than one month remaining in my tenure, a credible death threat was made against me by Palestinians in the Nablus region. The reason given for the threat, which was made not directly to me but to the UNRWA senior staff, was that I had been seen "chauffeuring an Israeli general" around town during a particularly violent period. This would have been my sister, on a short visit from the United States. I believe instead that my advocating for more women in positions of political power among the Palestinian hierarchy was the real reason for the threat. I was given a farewell party in Nablus anyway–on the top of Mount Gerizim, where Abraham nearly sacrificed Isaac.

Dedicated to Robin Roosevelt, fellow RAO (1954-1999)

Afterword

Many people have asked me how I changed because of this project, how reading some of the grim stories collected here affected me. Friends and family were concerned that I was so immersed in the hardships of wars and disasters that I could no longer enjoy life. And, in some sense, this is true; it was sometimes depressing to work with these stories. But it was also life-affirming in unexpected ways.

Though I have always been a political activist, I realized that my knowledge of international affairs was inadequate when I began this book. I wanted to learn more. As a consequence of this education, I do not see the world in the same way as I did two years ago. Newspaper articles and television news reports of conflict are now of special interest to me. As I write, inspections are taking place in Iraq. I wonder how many refugees there will be spilling out of that forlorn country after an American invasion and whether any of the relief workers I know will be there to receive them in camps. Like many people, I feel confused about the necessity of military action sometimes; I am not a pacifist–I would have wielded a gun against Hitler–yet I want to work for peace. How can this be achieved?

I was in New York on September 11, 2001, and was already deeply immersed in this project. For hours, my husband and I could not get in touch with our daughter, who lives on the other side of the city, or my elderly mother who lives outside the city. We walked down Second Avenue to the Red Cross to donate blood, dazed and shocked, stumbling into workers returning on foot from the site of the disaster, most of them covered in white ash. I was heartbroken at the horror of what had befallen us: New York City–my safe haven, my childhood home–had become a war zone. Days later I wrote a poem and recited it at a benefit for victims' families. But I also tried to look at the world outside America. I did not walk around the city waving an American flag, nor did I put an American flag pin on my lapel. I went to the bookstore at the United Nations and bought a UN pin. When people asked me why I wore it instead of an American flag, I said quietly some words I had recently read: "culture of peace."

It was not that my values have changed in any way–I was a participant in the anti-Vietnam war movement–but that I now understand that to work for peace must be a lifetime commitment beyond any one war, or any one terrorist attack, and that to support the United Nations is an important component of this commitment. I make no apologies for these idealistic sentiments, which have strengthened in the months I have been compiling and editing *Another Day in Paradise*. But even for me, a writer and a teacher of writing, words are not enough. I knew I had to do something more right away. After some thought, I volunteered with a refugee resettlement agency in New York, where I am mentoring Ozrenka, a refugee from Bosnia. If I were younger and did not have family obligations, I probably would become a humanitarian or human rights worker, and volunteer for a field assignment. But I cannot. So my one hour a week with Ozrenka has to be enough. When I am with her, I think of my own mother, who also escaped genocide as a refugee. Humanitarian workers helped her at the most dire moment of her life, and now I am returning the favor, even though I know my contribution is limited, that whatever I do for Ozrenka and she does for me, there was still a war, and that war went on for four excruciating years.

And I suppose this is something else I have learned: Humanitarian workers cannot prevent disaster or war; their role is confined to helping the victims. That said, their witnessing presence in the field is an important one. It should not be underestimated, disregarded, or obliterated by polemical discussions about the "aid business" and all its failings. In truth, there isn't anything anyone can say or write about the imperfect system in which humanitarian workers operate that will change my opinion about them as people; they are an inspiring bunch.

In mid-November of 2002–the book already in production–I attended a debate sponsored by the Department of Public Information at the United Nations. The audience–humanitarian workers, UN notables, representatives of NGOs–had come to hear David Rieff, author of *A Bed for the Night: Humanitarianism in Crisis*, present his excoriating critique of the international emergency-relief system. Rieff is considered by many to be the enfant terrible of war reporters, with a special interest in humanitarian assistance. He has seen a lot of awful things, and he writes thoughtfully. But he has very few, if any, solutions. The world is getting worse, not better, Rieff says. Even if he is right—and I don't think he is—I cannot abide his skepticism about humanitarian work in the field, or in the refugee camps, where people are hurting. I think this "right" action, as the Buddhists would say, has a cumulative long-range benefit and should not be dismissed so easily.

A day after the UN conference, John le Carré's foreword to this book arrived, an eloquent antidote to David Rieff's pessimism. I then read through *Another Day in Paradise* again. There isn't a story in this collection where working for a more peaceful and equitable world isn't a motivating imperative.

And so I confess I haven't been able to abandon entirely my romantic notions of humanitarian work, though they have been tempered by the gritty, real-time stories in this anthology. The tempering was both educative and necessary as I made my imaginative foray into the field through the manuscripts I was editing. I had to develop a callus—like the workers themselves—in order to read the stories day after day.

This is one way that the humanitarian workers survive the atrocities and suffering they witness; this is how they continue working. They have to distance themselves a bit, develop a protective, functional shield. Not surprisingly, therefore, it is sometimes difficult for them to admit vulnerability when writing about an experience. I struggled, often at long distance, to make them feel safe enough to do this, to let their in-the-field personae down a bit. I think, for the most part, that I have succeeded. I know that the workers themselves felt a catharsis using their own distinctive voices, rather than the omniscient voice of aid agency reports they are asked to produce. I am pleased that they have had a chance to speak freely to a wider audience about their frequently misunderstood profession.

Acknowledgments

I am indebted above all to the humanitarian workers who have generously entrusted me with their stories for this book.

When the anthology was still an idea, and I knew very little about the aid industry, Iain Levine, Maria Blacque-Belair, John Fawcett, MacKay Wolff, and Jane Springer patiently mentored and encouraged me. Without them this book would not have happened. My thanks, also, to Joel Charny and Dr. Jennifer Walser for allowing me to use their stories for the proposal.

Jennifer Wilder at Oxfam (US), Rudy Von Bernuth at Save the Children (US), Kim Gordon Bates at the International Committee for the Red Cross (ICRC), Jennifer Lindsey at Catholic Relief Services (CRS), and Austen Davies at Médecins Sans Frontières (MSF) Holland were particularly supportive. A special thanks to the ICRC staff members at Versoix, Switzerland, for their hospitality, especially the "two Dominiques," and to Juan Martinez and Eros Bosisio for their guidance and companionship during field day.

I want also to thank the following people, who helped me in one way or another with personal support and encouragement, research and/or critiquing of the manuscript: Harmer Johnson in New York, Norma Cohen in London, Sandy Duncan, and Marilyn and Ian Wood on Gabriola Island, B.C. To George and Kit Szanto in their idyll on Gabriola, a very special hug and thanks.

And for others who responded rapidly, graciously, and with interest to requests for information, and contacts, my gratitude: Scott Anderson, Michael Maren, Ambassador Morton Abramowitz, Congressman Steven Solarz, Christiane Amanpour, Dennis King at the US government's Humanitarian Information Unit, Carol Skyrm at the International Center for Transitional Justice, who introduced me to Maria Blacque-Belair, John Walker, Caroline Howie at BBC Worldwide. A special thanks to Bruce Hunter and John le Carré for their enthusiasm.

Most of the photographs in this book have been donated, either by the humanitarian workers themselves, the agencies, or photographers for the agencies. Special thanks for their help in locating and/or providing images to Mike Wells (Save the Children-UK); Mr. Reyes at the UN Photo Library in New York; Susan Hopper, photo editor at UNHCR in Geneva; Nigel Robinson at Halo Trust, Inc., in New York; Ellen Tolmie, photography editor at UNICEF in New York; Amani Shaltout, UNRWA photo librarian in Gaza; Catherine Kovacs at the WFP Photo Unit.

To work in isolation without friends and family is impossible for any writer/editor. My husband, Jim, has been there every morning, every night, through all the travails, and joys, of this project. He scanned photos, solved computer problems, was there, always. So, too, my mother. She read the manuscript as she was turning ninety years old with the enthusiasm of the dynamic young woman she has always been. My daughter, Chloe, is an inspiration.

For their interest, encouragement, and stimulating conversation during the months when this book was in progress, I would like to thank Adrienne Alicea and Pierre Kahn, Dr. Nabila El-Bessel and Ahmed Khandra, Mel and Zuleika Henry, Gene Koretz and Sylvia Borget, Bibi Brown, Sue Bernstein, Anne Bergman, Burke Walker, Paulette Licitra and Peter Selgin, Ladan Akbarnia, Barrie Balter, Michael Collins, Millie Gregory, Suzanne Vreeland, Bob Garber, Judy Johnson, Valerie Kaye, Justin Schlicht, Bryan Merton, Rashid Sherif, Sylvia Simmons Neumann, Osni Kezra, Mildred and Gerry Oppenheimer, Nick Peim, Linda Broughton, Carol and John Tateishi, Carmen Tan, Joan Stern, Barbara Walker, Barbi and Fred Poll, Peggy and Randy Weis, Linda Esposito, Saundra Segan, Marjorie Moser at the IRC Refugee Resettlement Program, and Irene and Phil Tufano.

Heartfelt thanks to Ezra Fitz at RLR Associates; to Robert Ellsberg, my steadfast editor, Catherine Costello, production coordinator, and Roberta Savage, art director at Orbis Books; to Jonathan Sinclair Wilson, Victoria Burrows, and Rob West at Earthscan Books; and to my agent, Jennifer Unter, who never lost hope that this book would be published.

Contributors

Paul E. Arès is a Canadian who joined the World Food Program (WFP) of the United Nations in 1991. Earlier in his career, he studied opera for a number of years and was active in promoting bilingualism and French Canadian culture in Canada. He was also involved in the restoration of historical buildings and sites and was director of the Property Program for Heritage Canada. Prior to joining the UN, he was a deputy director in the International Programs Branch at Agriculture Canada. In the WFP, he has occupied the posts of chief of resources and then chief of programming before taking up the post of WFP regional manager for West Africa in 1997. In 2000, he worked as associate director to the UN Development Group Office in New York on loan from the WFP. He is now deputy regional director for the WFP in Latin America and the Caribbean.

Carol Bergman (compiler and editor), a child of refugees from genocide, grew up in New York City. Both of her parents are physicians who worked for the Red Cross in Paris as they awaited their visas to the United States. She received her BA from the University of California at Berkeley and her MA from The New School University. Together with her husband, Jim, she lived in London for ten years, where she worked as an educator and journalist. Her fiction and nonfiction have appeared in numerous publications in both the UK and the United States. "Objects of Desire," which appeared in *Whetstone Literary Review* and *Lilith,* was nominated for the 1999 Pushcart Prize in Nonfiction. A memoir, *Searching for Fritzi,* was published that same year by Mediacs Press. Bergman teaches writing at New York University and is working on a novel and a collection of novellas.

Theresa Baldini, M.M., was born in Brooklyn, New York. After high school she worked on Wall Street as a secretary for about two years. In 1955, she entered the Maryknoll Sisters in Maryknoll, New York. She was assigned to the Contemplative Community with Maryknoll in 1963. Her first mission was on the Navajo Reservation on the outskirts of Gallup, New Mexico. From 1986 to

1992, Sister Theresa and Sister Madeline (McHugh) ran a house in South Sudan for African Sisters desiring the contemplative life. When the government army advanced on the rebel-held territory of Torit, the sisters were forced to flee with the local people. As the population moved, so did the bishop of Torit and others in the diocese, including Sisters Theresa and Madeline. In January 2000, they joined the growing community of displaced people in Narus where they still live today in their house of prayer and peace.

Maria Blacque-Belair grew up in Morocco and the United States. From 1992 to 1996 she worked in Sarajevo for the International Rescue Committee (IRC) and Action Internationale Contre la Faim (AICF). She has also served as a humanitarian worker in Romania, Iraq, and Rwanda. Upon returning from the field, she completed an MSW degree, with a specialty in trauma and recovery, at New York University. She currently works as a psychosocial counselor for refugees at the New York–based agency Solace/Safe Horizon. She is the founder of the Refugee and Immigrant Fund. Maria and her husband, John Fawcett, whom she met in the field, returned to a peaceful Sarajevo for their wedding in the summer of 1999. They are currently raising twins, a boy and girl named Sami and Maia.

Christine Darcas received a BA from Wesleyan University in African studies and political science before she worked for USAID/Chad from 1984 to 1986. After returning to the United States, she married François-Xavier Darcas, a French relief worker she had met in Chad, and earned her MBA from Cornell University. From 1984 to 1993, she worked at Lever Brothers in New York City, where she became product manager for the company's tallow bar group in the United States. When François's career involved a move to Hong Kong, she decided to devote her time to raising her family. Through subsequent moves to France and Australia, she has cared for her two children, volunteered in local communities, and pursued a career as a writer. Her stories have been published in the United States, Hong Kong, and France. She recently finished her first novel. She is currently in the postgraduate writing program at Deakin University in Melbourne, Australia.

Marleen Deerenberg was born in Amsterdam, Holland. She was educated as a social worker. When she realized that it would be difficult to find a posting in relief work abroad in that profession, she decided to obtain a degree in business administration. She worked as an administrator for Médecins Sans Frontières (MSF) in Albania and Afghanistan and stayed on in Afghanistan with HealthNet International, founded by MSF, but now an independent agency. After six years abroad, she returned to Holland to start taking lessons in creative writing. She is currently working on a novel set in Afghanistan and working part-time in the MSF office in Amsterdam. She returned to Peshawar, Pakistan, in November 2001 to help sort out expatriates' accounts after the evacuation. She found the Afghan people homeless and destitute, awaiting their fate in refugee camps, as in 1995, when she first arrived there.

Patrick Dillon was born in New York City's Hell's Kitchen. He was educated at the University of Notre Dame (political theory) and Pratt Institute (drawing, painting, and film). He served as a medic in Southeast Asia during the last year of the Vietnam War and in the Peace Corps in Thailand in malaria control immediately after the war. He is a novelist, journalist, and filmmaker, whose reportage has appeared in *The Village Voice, The Amsterdam News,* and *First of the Month Magazine.* His documentary "Inferno–Ethnic Cleansing from Kosovo to Harlem" is now in post-production. His new film, "Raining Planes," about the CIA's involvement in the World Trade Towers attack, is shooting in New York and California. Mr. Dillon lives and works in Harlem, where for the last thirteen years he has worked with HIV-positive and substance-addicted newborns.

Dr. Panayotis A. Ellinas grew up in a refugee camp in Cyprus in the 1970s. This camp is still in existence today, and the exhumation of mass graves on the still-divided island by human rights monitors continues. Despite childhood hardship, Pani (as he is known to his family and friends) was a good student. He received a scholarship to Swarthmore College in the United States and then to the Albert Einstein College of Medicine in the Bronx. Later, he lived in Tucson and received a degree in public health from the University of Arizona. He holds American Specialty Residency Training in both radiation oncology and preventive medicine. After his mission in Cambodia, he served in Albania during the war in Kosovo as a medical coordinator for the International Rescue Committee (IRC). He was a project manager for the World Health Organization's Humanitarian Action, Emergency Preparedness and Response Unit in Albania until 2002. He has recently married and become the proud father of a baby boy.

Philippe Gaillard grew up in the southern part of Switzerland. He studied French and German literature with a special focus on the medieval period, "just to be updated," he says. He has been working for the International Committee of the Red Cross (ICRC) since 1982 in many areas of conflict: Iraq, Argentina, Chile Uruguay, Paraguay, El Salvador, Colombia, Ecuador, Venezuela, Surinam, Rwanda, Lebanon, Mexico and Croatia. Philippe and his wife, Maria Teresa, met in Colombia in 1988. They have two children: Benjamin, born in Beirut on 20 April 1995, and Isabel, born also on 20 April in Mexico City in 1997. Between 1991 and 2001, Philippe spent all his free time restoring a medieval house in Saint-Pierre-de-Clages, a small village with five hundred inhabitants and one of the best vineyards in Switzerland, especially known for its Syrah and Johannisberg. He is currently working for the ICRC in Lima, Peru.

Henry Gaudru was born and raised in Paris. He studied geology with a special focus on volcanic phenomena. He has visited all the notorious active volcanoes in the world and observed many eruptions. Since 1991, he has been president of the European Volcanological Society based in Geneva, Switzerland. He is also a member of the International Commission on Mitigation of Volcanic Disasters (IAVCEI). From 1990 to 1999, he worked for the UN's International Decade for Natural Disaster Reduction (IDNDR), traveling to Cape Verde, Cameroon, Ecuador, the West Indies, and many other countries. Since 2000, he has been working with a new UN program, the International Strategy for Disasters Reduction (ISDR). He has published books and articles about volcanoes for the general public, including *Des Volcans et Des Hommes* (Men and Volcanoes), Tricorne Press, 1997. Currently, he is working on a television program about volcanic eruptions.

Paul Heslop, former vice-president, HALO:USA, earned a bachelor's degree from the University of Cranfield, UK, and the Royal Military Academy at Sandhurst, where he became a commissioned officer in the British Army. He began working for the Halo Trust in 1994. He has personally cleared over two thousand mines and thirty thousand unexploded (UXO) rockets, mortars, grenades, and bombs in Mozambique, Kosovo, Cambodia, Laos, Afghanistan, and Angola.

Iain Levine was born in Bradford, England. He trained as a nurse and began his overseas career in Calcutta, India, in a home for the destitute dying run by the Missionaries of Charity. He then worked for ten years in humanitarian programs for Save the Children Fund (UK) and UNICEF in north and south Sudan and Mozambique. He moved to New York in 1996, where he worked as Amnesty International's representative to the United Nations and then as chief of humanitarian policy and advocacy for UNICEF. He is now program director with Human Rights Watch.

Ngan Thuy Nguyen was born in Vietnam and immigrated with her family to New Orleans after the fall of Saigon in 1975. After graduation from Tulane University, she was awarded a Thomas J. Watson fellowship, which enabled her to travel throughout Southeast Asia to conduct gender and development research. This was the first time she had returned to Vietnam since her departure as a four-year-old child. The research led to several assignments with UNESCO and UNICEF-Vietnam, where she was the first overseas Vietnamese to work in their Hanoi office. After acquiring a master's degree at the Fletcher School of Law and Diplomacy, she joined the Harvard Institute for International Development and then Oxfam America. Ngan and her husband live in London where she is completing her doctorate in Mekong River resource management at The School of Oriental and African Studies.

John Sifton is a human rights attorney and writer who grew up in Brooklyn, New York. After graduation from St. John's College in Annapolis, Maryland, he studied international law at New York University School of Law while working in the International

Human Rights Clinic. During the spring and summer of 1999, he traveled to Albania and Kosovo working for Refugees International and the United Nations Development Program (UNDP). After graduation, he worked as a humanitarian aid worker in Pakistan and Afghanistan and later as a consultant for Human Rights Watch. He returned to Afghanistan in 2002 to prepare a report on civilian casualties during US-led military operations 2001-2002. He is based in New York City.

David Snyder was born and raised in Baltimore, Maryland, and educated in the United States. He has a bachelor's degree in English from Washington College and a master's degree in professional writing from Towson State University. He began his career with Catholic Relief Services (CRS) in 1996, working in the agency's Communications Department before accepting a three-month temporary duty assignment in 1999 during the Kosovo crisis. From there, he joined the agency's Emergency Response Team in Nairobi, Kenya, where he still lives. He has traveled extensively to conflict and disaster zones around the world, including Timor, Sudan, Pakistan, Kosovo, India, Congo, and Sierra Leone.

MacKay Wolff was born in Baltimore, Maryland. His father is a physician and all of his four siblings are engaged in altruistic work. He attended Oberlin College, where he studied music, philosophy, and religion; his graduate work in economics and political science was completed at the School for Advanced International Studies in Washington, D.C. He has been a humanitarian worker for more than twenty years and has been a staff member of the United Nations since 1989. Starting as a human rights observer with the United Nations Relief and Works Agency for Palestine Refugees (UNRWA) in the West Bank, where his piece is set, he has also served as a program officer in Turkey, Iraq, Bosnia, Rwanda, and Albania. In 1999, he was named coordinator of a new initiative for women and children with UNICEF. Currently, he is working as a speechwriter and writer for the UN in New York City.

Aid Agencies

The following is a list of some international humanitarian organizations. There are several other United Nations agencies, independent international agencies, and nongovernmental agencies. More than one thousand NGOs are registered in Afghanistan. For a complete listing of humanitarian relief agencies, see www.reliefweb.org.

International Agencies

ICRC: The International Committee of the Red Cross was established in 1863 after the Crimean War. The ICRC is an independent and neutral organization that serves all vulnerable persons—wounded, civilians, prisoners of war—caught up in a conflict. The ICRC is mandated by the international community to defend and promote the Geneva Conventions and is therefore considered to be a particularly relevant provider of legal advice where the applicability of international humanitarian law may be in question. It has observer status at the UN. www.icrc.org

IDNDR: The International Decade for Natural Disaster sReduction is a consortium of international organizations formed in response to a 1993 UN resolution. Its mandate is to mitigate natural disasters and to raise the level of awareness about natural disasters. www.unisdr.org

UNICEF: The United Nations Children's Fund was created by the UN General Assembly in 1946, after World War II, to help children. Today, it is involved in development work and the protection of children in the midst of war and natural disasters. www.unicef.org

UNHCR: The Office of the United Nations High Commissioner for Refugees was established on December 14, 1950, by the United Nations General Assembly. The agency is mandated to lead and coordinate international action to protect refugees and to resolve refugee problems worldwide. Its primary purpose is to safeguard the rights and well-being of refugees. It strives to ensure that everyone can exercise the right to seek asylum and to find safe refuge in another state, with the option to return home voluntarily, integrate locally, or resettle in a third country. In more than five decades the agency has helped an estimated fifty million people restart their lives. Today, a staff of around five thousand people in more than 120 countries continues to help an estimated 19.8 million persons. www.unhcr.ch

UNRWA: The UN Relief and Works Agency for Palestine Refugees in the Near East was established following the 1948 Arab-Israeli conflict. UNRWA is mandated to carry out direct relief and works programs for Palestinian refugees. In the absence of a settlement, the mandate has been repeatedly renewed. It is now extended until June 2005. www.un.org/unrwa

WFP: The World Food Program, set up in 1963 to fight global hunger, has in recent years become an emergency relief organization. www.wfp.org

WHO: The World Health Organization was set up to provide medical treatment as well as mental and social well-being. www.who.int/en

Nongovernmental Organizations

AMNESTY INTERNATIONAL is a worldwide campaigning movement that works to promote internationally recognized human rights. www.amnesty.org

ARC: American Refugee Committee. Founded in 1978 by a Chicago businessman, ARC is active in primary health care delivery and development in Africa, Asia, and Europe. www.archq.org

AICF: Action Internationale Contre la Faim (Action Against Hunger) was founded in 1979 by a group of French writers and intellectuals. It specializes in famine relief and global hunger. www.acf-fr.org

CRS: Catholic Relief Services, the official US Catholic relief organization, is dedicated to assisting the poor in other countries. www.catholicrelief.org

CONCERN: Concern Worldwide was founded in 1968 during the Nigerian Civil War and is currently based in Ireland. It is devoted to relief assistance and development in the poor world. www.concern.ie

HALO TRUST: The Halo Trust pioneered the concept of humanitarian landmine clearance in Afghanistan in 1988. During 2000, the organization cleared 246,689 explosive items in more than a dozen countries. www.halotrust.org

HEALTHNET INTERNATIONAL: Based in the Netherlands, Healthnet International was established by Médecins Sans Frontières in 1992 to bridge the gap between humanitarian relief and structural support for health services in war-affected countries. www.healthnetinternational.org

HUMAN RIGHTS WATCH: Human Rights Watch is an independent investigative organization that challenges governments to uphold international law. www.hrw.org

IRC: The International Rescue Committee, one of the largest American NGOs, was founded during World War II to help refugees escape from occupied France. It also resettles refugees in the United States. www.theIRC.org

MSF/Médecins Sans Frontières (Doctors without Borders): This is the largest independent medical relief agency in the world. It was founded in 1971 by a group of French doctors working for the ICRC during the Nigerian Civil War. It received the Nobel Prize in 1999. www.msf.org

OXFAM: The Oxford Committee for Famine Relief was founded in 1942 as a response to starvation in Nazi-occupied Greece. Today Oxfam is active in reform of international trade, human rights, debt relief, and development, as well as emergency relief. www.oxfam.org.uk or www.oxfamamerica.org

SCF: Save the Children Fund was founded in Britain after World War I to serve the starving children in Austria and Germany. It has expanded its mandate to include human rights work, emergency relief, and social activism. www.savethechildren.org

Government Agencies

ECHO: The European Commission Humanitarian Aid Office was established by the European Union in 1992 to provide emergency assistance and relief to victims outside the European Union. It has the distinction of being the largest single donor in the world. europa.eu.int/comm./echo/en

USAID: The US Agency for International Development funds both development and emergency relief. After ECHO, it is the second largest donor in the world. www.usaid.gov